Legends of Maui

Legends of Maui
W.D. Westervelt

MINT EDITIONS

Legends of Maui was first published in 1910.

This edition published by Mint Editions 2021.

ISBN 9781513299563 | E-ISBN 9781513223841

Published by Mint Editions®

MINT
EDITIONS

minteditionbooks.com

Publishing Director: Jennifer Newens
Design & Production: Rachel Lopez Metzger
Project Manager: Micaela Clark
Typesetting: Westchester Publishing Services

Contents

PREFACE

M aui is a demi god whose name should probably be pronounced Ma-u-i, *i. e.*, Ma-oo-e. The meaning of the word is by no means clear. It may mean "to live," "to subsist." It may refer to beauty and strength, or it may have the idea of "the left hand" or "turning aside." The word is recognized as belonging to remote Polynesian antiquity.

MacDonald, a writer of the New Hebrides Islands, gives the derivation of the name Maui primarily from, the Arabic word "Mohyi," which means "causing to: live" or "life," applied sometimes to the gods and sometimes to chiefs as "preservers and sustainers" of their followers.

The Maui story probably contains a larger number of unique and ancient myths than that of any other legendary character in the mythology of any nation.

There are three centers for these legends, New Zealand in the south, Hawaii in the north, and the Tahitian group including the Hervey Islands in the east. In each of these groups of islands, separated by thousands of miles, there are the same legends, told in almost the same way, and with very little variation in names. The intermediate groups of islands of even as great importance as Tonga, Fiji or Samoa, possess the same legends in more or less of a fragmentary condition, as if the three centers had been settled first when the Polynesians were driven away from the Asiatic coasts by their enemies, the Malays. From these centers voyagers sailing away in search of adventures would carry fragments rather than complete legends. This is exactly what has been done and there are as a result a large number of hints of wonderful deeds. The really long legends as told about the demi god Ma-u-i and his mother Hina number about twenty.

It is remarkable that these legends have kept their individuality. The Polynesians are not a very clannish people. For some centuries they have not been in the habit of frequently visiting each other. They have had no written language, and picture writing of any kind is exceedingly rare throughout Polynesia and yet in physical traits, national customs, domestic habits, and language, as well as in traditions and myths, the different inhabitants of the islands of Polynesia are as near of kin as the cousins of the United States and Great Britain.

The Maui legends form one of the strongest links in the mythological chain of evidence which binds the scattered inhabitants of the Pacific into one nation. An incomplete list aids in making clear the fact that groups of islands hundreds and even thousands of miles apart have been peopled centuries past by the same organic race. Either complete or fragmentary Maui legends are found in the single islands and island groups of Aneityum, Bowditch or Fakaofa, Efate, Fiji, Fotuna, Gilbert, Hawaii, Hervey, Huahine, Mangaia, Manihiki, Marquesas, Marshall, Nauru, New Hebrides, New Zealand, Samoa, Savage, Tahiti or Society, Tauna, Tokelau and Tonga.

S. Percy Smith of New Zealand in his book Hawaiki mentions a legend according to which Maui made a voyage after overcoming a sea monster, visiting the Tongas, the Tahitian group, Vai-i or Hawaii, and the Paumotu Islands. Then Maui went on to U-peru, which Mr. Smith says "may be Peru." It was said that Maui named some of the islands of the Hawaiian group, calling the island Maui "Maui-ui in remembrance of his efforts in lifting up the heavens," Hawaii was named Vai-i, and Lanai was called Ngangai—as if Maui had found the three most southerly islands of the group.

The Maui legends possess remarkable antiquity. Of course, it is impossible to give any definite historical date, but there can scarcely be any question of their origin among the ancestors of the Polynesians before they scattered over the Pacific ocean. They belong to the prehistoric Polynesians. The New Zealanders claim Maui as an ancestor of their most ancient tribes and sometimes class him among the most ancient of their gods, calling him "creator of land" and "creator of man." Tregear, in a paper before the New Zealand Institute, said that Maui was sometimes thought to be "the sun himself," "the solar fire," "the sun god," while his mother Hina was called "the moon goddess." The noted greenstone god of the Maoris of New Zealand, Potiki, may well be considered a representation of Maui-Tiki-Tiki, who was sometimes called Maui-po-tiki.

Whether these legends came to the people in their sojourn in India before they migrated to the Straits of Sunda is not certain; but it may well be assumed that these stories had taken firm root in the memories of the priests who transmitted the most important traditions from generation to generation, and that this must have been done before they were driven away from the Asiatic coasts by the Malays.

Several hints of Hindoo connection is found in the Maui legends. The Polynesians not only ascribed human attributes to all animal life with which they were acquainted, but also carried the idea of an alligator or dragon with them, wherever they went, as in the mo-o of the story Tuna-roa.

The Polynesians also had the idea of a double soul inhabiting the body. This is carried out in the ghost legends more fully than in the Maui stories, and yet "the spirit separate from the spirit which never forsakes man" according to Polynesian ideas, was a part of the Maui birth legends. This spirit, which can be separated or charmed away from the body by incantations was called the "hau," When Maui's father performed the religious ceremonies over him which would protect him and cause him to be successful, he forgot a part of his incantation to the "hau," therefore Maui lost his protection from death when he sought immortality for himself and all mankind.

How much these things aid in proving a Hindoo or rather Indian origin for the Polynesians is uncertain, but at least they are of interest along the lines of race origin.

The Maui group of legends is preminently peculiar. They are not only different from the myths of other nations, but they are unique in the character of the actions recorded. Maui's deeds rank in a higher class than most of the mighty efforts of the demi gods of other nations and races, and are usually of more utility. Hercules accomplished nothing to compare with "lifting the sky," "snaring the sun," "fishing for islands," "finding fire in his grandmother's fingernails," "learning from birds how to make fire by rubbing dry sticks," or "getting a magic bone" from the jaw of an ancestor who was half dead, that is dead on one side and therefore could well afford to let the bone on that side go for the benefit of a descendant. The Maui legends are full of helpful imaginations, which are distinctly Polynesian.

The phrase "Maui of the Malo" is used among the Hawaiians in connection with the name Maui a Kalana, "Maui the son of Akalana." It may be well to note the origin of the name. It was said that Hina usually sent her retainers to gather sea moss for her, but one morning she went down to the sea by herself. There she found a beautiful red malo, which she wrapped around her as a pa-u or skirt. When she showed it to Akalana, her husband, he spoke of it as a gift of the gods, thinking that it meant the gift of Maria or spiritual power to their child when he should be born. In this way the Hawaiians explain the superior talent and miraculous ability of Maui which placed him above his brothers.

These stories were originally printed as magazine articles, chiefly in the Paradise of the Pacific, Honolulu; therefore there are sometimes repetitions which it seemed best to leave, even when reprinted in the present form.

I

Maui's Home

"Akalana was the man;
Hira-a-ke-ahi was the wife;
Maui First was born;
Then Maui-waena;
Maui Kiikii was born;
Then Maui of the malo."

—Queen Liliuokalani's Family Chant

Four Brothers, each bearing the name of Maui, belong to Hawaiian legend. They accomplished little as a family, except on special occasions when the youngest of the household awakened his brothers by some unexpected trick which drew them into unwonted action. The legends of Hawaii, Tonga, Tahiti, New Zealand and the Hervey group make this youngest Maui "the discoverer of fire" or "the ensnarer of the sun" or "the fisherman who pulls up islands" or "the man endowed with magic," or "Maui with spirit power." The legends vary somewhat, of course, but not as much as might be expected when the thousands of miles between various groups of islands are taken into consideration.

Maui was one of the Polynesian demi-gods. His parents belonged to the family of supernatural beings. He himself was possessed of supernatural powers and was supposed to make use of all manner of enchantments. In New Zealand antiquity a Maui was said to have assisted other gods in the creation of man. Nevertheless Maui was very human. He lived in thatched houses, had wives and children, and was scolded by the women for not properly supporting his household.

The time of his sojourn among men is very indefinite. In Hawaiian genealogies Maui and his brothers were placed among the descendants of Ulu and "the sons of Kii," and Maui was one of the ancestors of Kamehameha, the first king of the united Hawaiian Islands. This would place him in the seventh or eighth century of the Christian Era. But it is more probable that Maui belongs to the mist-land of time. His mischievous pranks with the various gods would make him another

Mercury living in any age from the creation to the beginning of the Christian era.

The Hervey Island legends state that Maui's father was "the supporter of the heavens" and his mother "the guardian of the road to the invisible world."

In the Hawaiian chant, Akalana was the name of his father. In other groups this was the name by which his mother was known. Kanaloa, the god, is sometimes known as the father of Maui. In Hawaii Hina was his mother. Elsewhere Ina, or Hina, was the grandmother, from whom he secured fire.

The Hervey Island legends say that four mighty ones lived in the old world from which their ancestors came. This old world bore the name Ava-iki, which is the same as Hawa-ii, or Hawaii. The four gods were Mauike, Ra, Ru, and Bua-Taranga.

It is interesting to trace the connection of these four names with Polynesian mythology. Mauike is the same as the demi-god of New Zealand, Mafuike. On other islands the name is spelled Mauika, Mafuika, Mafuia, Mafuie, and Mahuika. Ra, the sun god of Egypt, is the same as Ra in New Zealand and La (sun) in Hawaii. Ru, the supporter of the heavens, is probably the Ku of Hawaii, and the Tu of New Zealand and other islands, one of the greatest of the gods worshiped by the ancient Hawaiians. The fourth mighty one from Ava-ika was a woman, Bua-taranga, who guarded the path to the underworld. Talanga in Samoa, and Akalana in Hawaii were the same as Taranga. Pua-kalana (the Kalana flower) would probably be the same in Hawaiian as Bua-taranga in the language of the Society Islands.

Ru, the supporter of the Heavens, married Buataranga, the guardian of the lower world. Their one child was Maui. The legends of Raro-Toaga state that Maui's father and mother were the children of Tangaroa (Kanaloa in Hawaiian), the great god worshiped throughout Polynesia. There were three Maui brothers and one sister, Ina-ika (Ina, the fish).

The New Zealand legends relate the incidents of the babyhood of Maui.

Maui was prematurely born, and his mother, not, caring to be troubled with him, cut off a lock of her hair, tied it around him and cast him into the sea. In this way the name came to him, Maui-Tiki-Tiki, or "Maui formed in the topknot." The waters bore him safely. The jelly fish enwrapped and mothered him. The god of the seas cared for and protected him. He was carried to the god's house and hung up in the roof that he inight feel the warm air of the fire, and be cherished into life. When he was old enough, he came to his relations while they were all gathered in the great House of Assembly, dancing and making merry. Little Maui crept in and sat down behind his brothers. Soon his mother called the children and found a strange child, who proved that he was her son, and was taken in as one of the family. Some of the brothers were jealous, but the eldest addressed the others as follows:

"Never mind; let him be our dear brother. In the days of peace remember the proverb, 'When you are on friendly terms, settle your disputes in a friendly way; when you are at war, you must redress your injuries by violence.' It is better for us, brothers, to be kind to other people. These are the ways by which men gain influence—by laboring for abundance of food to feed others, by collecting property to give to others, and by similar means by which you promote the good of others."

Thus, according to the New Zealand story related by Sir George Grey, Maui was received in his home.

Maui's home was placed by some of the Hawaiian myths at Kauiki, a foothill of the great extinct crater Haleakala, on the Island of Maui. It was here he lived when the sky was raised to its present position. Here was located the famous fort around which many battles were fought during the years immediately preceding the coming of Captain Cook. This fort was held by warriors of the Island of Hawaii a number of years. It was from this home that Maui was supposed to have journeyed when he climbed Mt. Haleakala to ensnare the sun.

And yet most of the Hawaiian legends place Maui's home by the rugged black lava beds of the Wailuku river near Hilo on the island Hawaii. Here he lived when he found the way to make fire by rubbing sticks together, and when he killed Kuna, the great eel, and performed other feats of valor. He was supposed to cultivate the land on the north side of the river. His mother, usually known as Hina, had her home in a lava cave under the beautiful Rainbow Falls, one of the fine scenic attractions of Hilo. An ancient demi-god, wishing to destroy this home, threw a great mass of lava across the stream below the falls. The rising water was fast filling the cave.

Hina called loudly to her powerful son Maui. He came quickly and found that a large and strong ridge of lava lay across the stream. One end rested against a small hill. Maui struck the rock on the other side of the hill and thus broke a new pathway for the river. The water swiftly flowed away and the cave remained as the home of the Maui family.

According to the King Kalakaua family legend, translated by Queen Liliuokalani, Maui and his brothers also made this place their home. Here he aroused the anger of two uncles, his mother's brothers, who were called "Tall Post" and "Short Post," because they guarded the entrance to a cave in which the Maui family probably had its home.

"They fought hard with Maui, and were thrown, and red water flowed freely from Maui's forehead. This was the first shower by Maui." Perhaps some family discipline followed this knocking down of door posts, for it is said:

> "They fetched the sacred Awa bush,
> Then came the second shower by Maui;
> The third shower was when the elbow of Awa was broken;
> The fourth shower came with the sacred bamboo."

Maui's mother, so says a New Zealand legend, had her home in the under-world as well as with her children. Maui determined to find the hidden dwelling place. His mother would meet the children in the evening and lie down to sleep with them and then disappear with the first appearance of dawn. Maui remained awake one night, and when all were asleep, arose quietly and stopped up every crevice by which a ray of light could enter. The morning came and the sun mounted up— far up in the sky. At last his mother leaped up and tore away the things which shut out the light.

"Oh, dear; oh, dear! She saw the sun high in the heavens; so she hurried away, crying at the thought of having been so badly treated by her own children."

Maui watched her as she pulled up a tuft of grass and disappeared in the earth, pulling the grass back to its place.

Thus Maui found the path to the under-world. Soon he transformed himself into a pigeon and flew down, through the cave, until he saw a party of people under a sacred tree, like those growing in the ancient first Hawaii. He flew to the tree and threw down berries upon the people. They threw back stones. At last he permitted a stone from his father to strike him, and he fell to the ground. "They ran to catch him but lo! the pigeon had turned into a man."

Then his father "took him to the water to be baptized" (possibly a modern addition to the legend). Prayers were offered and ceremonies passed through. But the prayers were incomplete and Maui's father knew that the gods would be angry and cause Maui's death, and all because in the hurried baptism a part of the prayers had been left unsaid. Then Maui returned to the upper world and lived again with his brothers.

Maui commenced his mischievous life early, for Hervey Islanders say that one day the children were playing a game dearly loved by Polynesians—hide-and-seek. Here a sister enters into the game and hides little Maui under a pile of dry sticks. His brothers could not find him, and the sister told them where to look. The sticks were carefully handled, but the child could not be found. He had shrunk himself so small that he was like an insect under some sticks and leaves. Thus early he began to use enchantments.

Maui's home, at the best, was only a sorry affair. Gods and demigods lived in caves and small grass houses. The thatch rapidly rotted and required continual renewal. In a very short time the heavy rains beat through the decaying roof. The home was without windows or doors, save as low openings in the ends or sides allowed entrance to those willing to crawl through. Off on one side would be the rude shelter, in the shadow of which Hina pounded the bark of certain trees into wood pulp and then into strips of thin, soft wood-paper, which bore the name of "Tapa cloth." This cloth Hina prepared for the clothing of Maui and his brothers. Tapa cloth was often treated to a coat of cocoa-nut, or candle-nut oil, making it somewhat waterproof and also more durable.

Here Maui lived on edible roots and fruits and raw fish, knowing little about cooked food, for the art of fire making was not yet known. In later years Maui was supposed to live on the eastern end of the island Maui, and also in another home on the large island Hawaii, on which he discovered how to make fire by rubbing dry sticks together. Maui was the Polynesian Mercury. As a little fellow he was endowed with peculiar powers, permitting him to become invisible or to change his human form into that of an animal. He was ready to take anything from any one by craft or force. Nevertheless, like the thefts of Mercury, his pranks usually benefited mankind.

It is a little curious that around the different homes of Maui, there is so little record of temples and priests and altars. He lived too far back for priestly customs. His story is the rude, mythical survival of the days when of church and civil government there was none and worship of the gods was practically unknown, but every man was a law unto himself, and also to the other man, and quick retaliation followed any injury received.

II

MAUI THE FISHERMAN

"Oh the great fish hook of Maui!
Manai-i-ka-lani 'Made fast to the heavens'—its name;
An earth-twisted cord ties the hook.
Engulfed from the lofty Kauiki.
Its bait the red billed Alae,
The bird made sacred to Hina.
It sinks far down to Hawaii,
Struggling and painfully dying.
Caught is the land under the water,
Floated up, up to the surface,
But Hina hid a wing of the bird
And broke the land under the water.
Below, was the bait snatched away
And eaten at once -by the fishes,
The Ulua of the deep muddy places."

—Chant of Kualii, about A.D. 1700

One of Maui's homes was near Kauiki, a place well known throughout the Hawaiian Islands because of its strategic importance. For many years it was the site of a fort around which fierce battles were fought by the natives of the island Maui, repelling the invasions of their neighbors from Hawaii.

Haleakala (the House of the Sun), the mountain from which Maui the demi-god snared the sun, looks down ten thousand feet upon the Kauiki headland. Across the channel from Haleakala rises Mauna Kea, "The White Mountain"—the snow-capped—which almost all the year round rears its white head in majesty among the clouds.

In the snowy breakers of the surf which washes the beach below these mountains, are broken coral reefs—the fishing grounds of the Hawaiians. Here near Kauiki, according to some Hawaiian legends, Maui's mother Hina had her grass house and made and dried her kapa cloth. Even to the present day it is one of the few places in the islands where the kapa is still pounded into sheets from the bark of the hibiscus and kindred trees.

Here is a small bay partially reef-protected, over which year after year the moist clouds float and by day and by night crown the waters with rainbows—the legendary sign of the home of the deified ones. Here when the tide is out the natives wade and swim, as they have done for centuries, from coral block to coral block, shunning the deep resting places of their dread enemy, the shark, sometimes esteemed divine. Out on the edge of the outermost reef they seek the shellfish which cling to the coral, or spear the large fish which have been left in the beautiful little lakes of the reef. Coral land is a region of the sea coast abounding in miniature lakes and rugged valleys and steep mountains. Clear waters with every motion of the tide surge in and out through sheltered caves and submarine tunnels, according to an ancient Hawaiian song—

"Never quiet, never failing, never sleeping,
Never very noisy is the sea of the sacred caves."

Sea mosses of many hues are the forests which drape the hillsides of coral land and reflect the colored rays of light which pierce the ceaselessly moving waves. Down in the beautiful little lakes, under overhanging coral cliffs, darting in and out through the fringes of seaweed, the purple mullet and royal red fish flash before the eyes of the fisherman. Sometimes the many-tinted glorious fish of paradise reveal their beauties, and then again a school of black and gold citizens of the reef follow the tidal waves around projecting crags and through the hidden tunnels from lake to lake, while above the fisherman follows spearing or snaring as best he can. Maui's brothers were better fishermen than he. They sought the deep sea beyond the reef and the larger fish. They made hooks of bone or of mother of pearl, with a straight, slender, sharp-pointed piece leaning backward at a sharp angle. This was usually a consecrated bit of bone or mother of pearl, and was supposed to have peculiar power to hold fast any fish which had taken the bait.

These bones were usually taken from the body of some one who while living had been noted for great power or high rank. This sharp piece was tightly tied to the larger bone or shell, which formed the shank of the hook. The sacred barb of Maui's hook was a part of the magic bone he had secured from his ancestors in the under-world—the bone with which he struck the sun while lassooing him and compelling him to move more slowly through the heavens.

"Earth-twisted"—fibres of vines—twisted while growing, was the cord used by Maui in tying the parts of his magic hook together.

Long and strong were the fish lines made from the olona fibre, holding the great fish caught from the depths of the ocean. The fibres of the olona vine were among the longest and strongest threads found in the Hawaiian Islands.

Such a hook could easily be cast loose by the struggling fish, if the least opportunity were given. Therefore it was absolutely necessary to keep the line taut, and pull strongly and steadily, to land the fish in the canoe.

Maui did not use his magic hook for a long time. He seemed to understand that it would not answer ordinary needs. Possibly the idea of making the supernatural hook did not occur to him until he had exhausted his lower wit and magic upon his brothers.

It is said that Maui was not a very good fisherman. Sometimes his end of the canoe contained fish which his brothers had thought were on their hooks until they were landed in the canoe.

Many times they laughed at him for his poor success, and he retaliated with his mischievous tricks.

"E!" he would cry, when one of his brothers began to pull in, while the other brothers swiftly paddled the canoe forward. "E!" See we both have caught great fish at the same moment. Be careful now. Your line is loose. Look out! Look out!"

All the time he would be pulling his own line in as rapidly as possible. Onward rushed the canoe. Each fisherman shouting to encourage the others. Soon the lines by the tricky manipulation of Maul would be crossed. Then as the great fish was brought near the side of the boat Maui the little, the mischievous one, would slip his hook toward the head of the fish and flip it over into the canoe—causing his brother's line to slacken for a moment. Then his mournful cry rang out: "Oh, my brother, your fish is gone. Why did you not pull more steadily? It was a fine fish, and now it is down deep in the waters." Then Maui held up his splendid catch (from his brother's hook) and received somewhat suspicious congratulations. But what could they do, Maui was the smart one of the family.

Their father and mother were both members of the household of the gods. The father was "the supporter of the heavens" and the mother was the guardian of the way to the invisible world," but pitifully small and very few were the gifts bestowed upon their children. Maui's brothers knew nothing beyond the average home life of the ordinary Hawaiian, and Maui alone was endowed with the power to work miracles. Nevertheless the student of Polynesian legends learns that Maui is more widely known than almost all the demi-gods of all nations as a discoverer of benefits for his fellows, and these physical rather than spiritual. After many fishing excursions Maui's brothers seemed to have wit enough to understand his tricks, and thenceforth they refused to take him in their canoe when they paddled out to the deep-sea fishing grounds. Then those who depended upon Maui to supply their daily needs murmured against his poor success. His mother scolded him and his brothers ridiculed him.

In some of the Polynesian legends it is said that his wives and children complained because of his laziness and at last goaded him into a new effort.

The ex-Queen Liliuokalani, in a translation of what is called "the family chant," says that Maui's mother sent him to his father for a hook with which to supply her need.

> *"Go hence to your father,*
> *'Tis there you find line and hook.*
> *This is the hook—'Made fast to the heavens—'*
> *'Manaia-ka-lani'—'tis called.*
> *When the hook catches land*
> *It brings the old seas together.*
> *Bring hither the large Alae,*
> *The bird of Hina.*

When Maui had obtained his hook, he tried to go fishing with his brothers. He leaped on the end of their canoe as they pushed out into deep water. They were angry and cried out: "This boat is too small for another Maui." So they threw him off and made him swim back to the beach. When they returned from their day's work, they brought back only a shark. Maui told them if he had been with them better fish would have been upon their hooks—the Ulua, for instance, or, possibly, the Pimoe—the king of fish. At last they let him go far out outside the harbor of Kipahula to a place opposite Ka Iwi o Pele, "The bone of Pele," a peculiar piece of lava lying near the beach at Hana on the eastern side of the island Maui. There they fished, but only sharks were caught. The brothers ridiculed Maui, saying: "Where are the Ulua, and where is Pimoe?"

Then Maui threw his magic hook into the sea, baited with one of the Alae birds, sacred to his mother Hina. He used the incantation, "When I let go my hook with divine power, then I get the great Ulua."

The bottom of the sea began to move. Great waves arose, trying to carry the canoe away. The fish pulled the canoe two days, drawing the line to its fullest extent. When the slack began to come in the line, because of the tired fish, Maui called for the brothers to pull hard against the coming fish. Soon land rose out of the water. Maui told them not to look back or the fish would be lost. One brother did look back—the line slacked, snapped, and broke, and the land lay behind them in islands.

One of the Hawaiian legends also says that while the brothers were paddling in full strength, Maui saw a calabash floating in the water. He lifted it into the canoe, and behold! his beautiful sister Hina of the sea. The brothers looked, and the separated islands lay behind them, free from the hook, while Cocoanut Island—the dainty spot of beauty in Hilo harbor—was drawn up-a little edge of lava—in later years the home of a cocoanut grove.

The better, the more complete, legend comes from New Zealand, which makes Maui so mischievous that his brothers refuse his companionship—and therefore, thrown on his own resources, he studies how to make a hook which shall catch something worth while. In this legend Maui is represented as making his own hook and then pleading with his brothers to let him go with them once more. But they hardened their hearts against him, and refused again and again.

Maui possessed the power of changing himself into different forms. At one time while playing with his brothers he had concealed himself for them to find. They heard his voice in a corner of the house—but could not find him. Then under the mats on the floor, but again they could not find him. There was only an insect creeping on the floor. Suddenly they saw their little brother where the insect had been. Then they knew he had been tricky with them. So in these fishing days he resolved to go back to his old ways and cheat his brothers into carrying him with them to the great fishing grounds.

Sir George Gray says that the New Zealand Maui went out to the canoe and concealed himself as an insect in the bottom of the boat so that when the early morning light crept over the waters and his brothers pushed the canoe into the surf they could not see him. They rejoiced that Maui did not appear, and paddled away over the waters.

They fished all day and all night and on the morning of the next day, out from among the fish in the bottom of the boat came their troublesome brother.

They had caught many fine fish and were satisfied, so thought to paddle homeward, but their younger brother plead with them to go out, far out, to the deeper seas and permit him to cast his hook. He said he wanted larger and better fish than any they had captured.

So they paddled to their outermost fishing grounds—but this did not satisfy Maui—

> *"Farther out on the waters,*
> *O! my brothers,*
> *I seek the great fish of the sea."*

It was evidently easier to work for him than to argue with him—therefore far out in the sea they went. The home land disappeared from view; they could see only the outstretching waste of waters. Maui urged them out still farther. Then he drew his magic hook from under his malo or loin-cloth. The brothers wondered what he would do for bait. The New Zealand legend says that he struck his nose a mighty blow until the blood gushed forth. When this blood became clotted, he fastened it upon his hook and let it down into the deep sea.

Down it went to the very bottom and caught the under world. It was a mighty fish—but the brothers paddled with all their might and main and Maui pulled in the line. It was hard rowing against the power which held the hook down in the sea depths—but the brothers became enthusiastic over Maui's large fish, and were generous in their strenuous endeavors. Every muscle was strained and every paddle held strongly against the sea that not an inch should be lost. There was no sudden leaping and darting to and fro, no "give" to the line; no "tremble" as when a great fish would shake itself in impotent wrath when held captive by a hook. It was simply a struggle of tense muscle against an immensely heavy dead weight. To the brothers there came slowly the feeling that Maui was in one of his strange moods and that something beyond their former experiences with their tricky brother was coming to pass.

At last one of the brothers glanced backward. With a scream of intense terror he dropped his paddle. The others also looked. Then each caught his paddle and with frantic exertion tried to force their canoe onward. Deep down in the heavy waters they pushed their paddles. Out of the great seas the black, ragged head of a large island was rising like a fish—it seemed to be chasing them, through the boiling surf. In a little while the water became shallow around them, and their canoe finally rested on a black beach.

Maui for some reason left his brothers, charging them not to attempt to cut up this great fish. But the unwise brothers thought they would fill the canoe with part of this strange thing which they had caught. They began to cut up the back and put huge slices into their canoe. But the great fish—the island—shook under the blows and with mighty earthquake shocks tossed the boat of the brothers, and their canoe was destroyed. As they were struggling in the waters, the great fish devoured them. The island came up more and more from the waters—but the deep gashes made by Maui's brothers did not heal—they became the mountains and valleys stretching from sea to sea.

White of New Zealand says that Maui went down into the underworld to meet his great ancestress, who was one side dead and one side alive. From the dead side he took the jaw bone, made a magic hook, and went fishing. When he let the hook down into the sea, he called:

> *"Take my bait. O Depths!*
> *Confused you are. O Depths!*
> *And coming upward."*

Thus he pulled up Ao-tea-roa—one of the large islands of New Zealand. On it were houses, with people around them. Fires were burning. Maui walked over the island, saw with wonder the strange men and the mysterious fire. He took fire in his hands and was burned. He leaped into the sea, dived deep, came up with the other large island on his shoulders. This island he set on fire and left it always burning, It is said that the name for New Zealand given to Captain Cook was Te ika o Maui, "The fish of Maui." Some New Zealand natives say that he fished up the island on which dwelt "Great Hina of the Night," who finally destroyed Maui while he was seeking immortality.

One legend says that Maui fished up apparently from New Zealand the large island of the Tongas. He used this chant:

"O Tonga-nui!
why art Thou
Sulkily biting, biting below!
Beneath the earth
The power is felt,
The foam is seen,
Coming.
O thou loved grandchild
Of Tangaro a-meha."

This is an excellent poetical description of the great fish delaying the quick hard bite. Then the island comes to the surface and Maui, the beloved grandchild of the Polynesian god Kanaloa, is praised.

It was part of one of the legends that Maui changed himself into a bird and from the heavens let down a line with which he drew up land, but the line broke, leaving islands rather than a mainland. About two hundred lesser gods went to the new islands in a large canoe. The greater gods punished them by making them mortal.

Turner, in his book on Samoa, says there were three Mauis, all brothers. They went out fishing from Rarotonga. One of the brothers begged the "goddess of the deep rocks" to let his hooks catch land. Then the island Manahiki was drawn up. A great wave washed two of the Mauis away. The other Maui found a great house in which eight hundred gods lived. Here he made his home until a chief from Rarotonga drove him away. He fled into the sky, but as he leaped he separated the land into two islands.

Other legends of Samoa say that Tangaroa, the great god, rolled stones from heaven. One became the island Savaii, the other became Upolu. A god is sometimes represented as passing over the ocean with a bag of sand. Wherever he dropped a little sand islands sprang up.

Payton, the earnest and honored missionary of the New Hebrides Islands, evidently did not know the name Mauitikitiki, so he spells the name of the fisherman Ma-tshi-ktshi-ki, and gives the myth of the fishing up of the various islands. The natives said that Maui left footprints on the coral reefs of each island where he stood straining and lifting in his endeavors to pull up each other island. He threw his line around a large island intending to draw it up and unite it with the one on which he stood, but his line broke. Then he became angry and divided into two parts the island on which he stood. This same Maui is recorded by Mr. Payton as being in a flood which put out one volcano—Maui seized another, sailed across to a neighboring island and piled it upon the top of the volcano there, so the fire was placed out of reach of the flood.

In the Hervey Group of the Tahitian or Society Islands the same story prevails and the natives point out the place where the hook caught and a print was made by the foot in the coral reef. But they add some very mythical details. Maui's magic fish hook is thrown into the skies, where it continuously hangs, the curved tail of the constellation which we call Scorpio. Then one of the gods becoming angry with Maui seized him and threw him also among the stars. There he stays looking down upon his people. He has become a fixed part of the scorpion itself.

The Hawaiian myths sometimes represent Maui as trying to draw the islands together while fishing them out of the sea. When they had pulled up the island of Kauai they looked back and were frightened. They evidently tried to rush away from the new monster and thus broke the line. Maui tore a side out of the small crater Kaula when trying to draw it to one of the other islands. Three aumakuas, three fishes supposed to be spirit-gods, guarded Kaula and defeated his purpose. At Hawaii Cocoanut Island broke off because Maui pulled too hard. Another place near Hilo on the large island of Hawaii where the hook was said to have caught is in the Wailuku river below Rainbow Falls.

Maui went out from his home at Kauiki, fishing with his brothers. After they had caught some fine fish the brothers desired to return, but Maui persuaded them to go out farther. Then when they became tired and determined to go back, he made the seas stretch out and the shores recede until they could see no land. Then drawing the magic hook, he baited it with the Alae or sacred mud hen belonging to his Mother Hina. Queen Liliuokalani's family chant has the following reference to this myth:

> *"Maui longed for fish for Hina-akeahi (Hina of the fire, his mother),*
> *Go hence to your father,*
> *There you will find line and hook.*
> *Manaiakalani is the hook.*
> *Where the islands are caught,*
> *The ancient seas are connected.*
> *The great bird Alae is taken,*

The sister bird,
Of that one of the hidden fire of Maui."

Maui evidently had no scruples against using anything which would help him carry out his schemes.

He indiscriminately robbed his friends and the gods alike.

Down in the deep sea sank the hook with its struggling bait, until it was seized by "the land under the water."

But Hina the mother saw the struggle of her sacred bird and hastened to the rescue. She caught a wing of the bird, but could not pull the Alae from the sacred hook. The wing was torn off. Then the fish gathered around the bait and tore it in pieces. If the bait could have been kept entire, then the land would have come up in a continent rather than as an island. Then the Hawaiian group would have been unbroken. But the bait broke-and the islands came as fragments from the under world.

Maui's hook and canoe are frequently mentioned in the legends. The Hawaiians have a long rock in the Wailuku river at Hilo which they call Maui's canoe. Different names were given to Maui's canoe by the Maoris of New Zealand. "Vine of Heaven," "Prepare for the North," "Land of the Receding Sea." His fish hook bore the name "Plume of Beauty."

On the southern end of Hawke's Bay, New Zealand, there is a curved ledge of rocks extending out from, the coast. This is still called by the Maoris "Maui's fish-hook," as if the magic hook had been so firmly caught in the jaws of the island that Maui could not disentangle it, but had been compelled to cut it off from his line.

There is a large stone on the sea coast of North Kohala on the island of Hawaii which the Hawaiians point out as the place where Maui's magic hook caught the island and pulled it through the sea.

In the Tonga Islands, a place known as Hounga is pointed out by the natives as the spot where the magic hook caught in the rocks. The hook itself was said to have been in the possession of a chief-family for many generations.

Another group of Hawaiian legends, very incomplete, probably referring to Maui, but ascribed to other names, relates that a fisherman caught a large block of coral. He took it to his priest. After sacrificing, and consulting the gods, the priest advised the fisherman to throw the coral back into the sea with incantations. While so doing this block became Hawaii-loa. The fishing continued and blocks of coral were caught and thrown back into the sea until all the islands appeared. Hints of this legend cling to other island groups as well as to the Hawaiian Islands. Fornander credits a fisherman from foreign lands as thus bringing forth the Hawaiian Islands from the deep seas. The reference occurs in part of a chant known as that of a friend of Paao—the priest who is supposed to have come from, Samoa to Hawaii in the eleventh century. This priest calls for his companions:

> *"Here are the canoes. Get aboard.*
> *Come along, and dwell on Hawaii with the green back.*
> *A land which was found in the ocean,*
> *A land thrown up from the sea—*
> *From the very depths of Kanaloa,*
> *The white coral, in the watery caves,*
> *That was caught on the hook of the fisherman."*

The god Kanaloa is sometimes known as a ruler of the under-world, whose land was caught by Maui's hook and brought up in islands. Thus in the legends the thought has been perpetuated that some one of the ancestors of the Polynesians made voyages and discovered islands.

In the time of Umi, King of Hawaii, there is the following record of an immense bone fish-hook, which was called the "fish-hook of Maui:"

"In the night of Mukti (the last night of the month), a priest and his servants took a man, killed him, and fastened his body to the hook, which bore the name Manai-a-ka-lani, and dragged it to the heiau (temple) as a 'fish,' and placed it on the altar."

This hook was kept until the time of Kamehameha I From time to time he tried to break it, and pulled until he perspired.

Peapea, a brother of Kaahumanu, took the hook and broke it. He was afraid that Kamehameha would kill him. Kaahumanu, however, soothed the King, and he passed the matter over. The broken bone was probably thrown away.

III

Maui Lifting the Sky

Maui's home was for a long time enveloped by darkness. The heavens had fallen down, or, rather, had not been separated from the earth.

According to some legends, the skies pressed so closely and so heavily upon the earth that when the plants began to grow, all the leaves were necessarily flat. According to other legends, the plants had to push up the clouds a little, and thus caused the leaves to flatten out into larger surface, so that they could better drive the skies back and hold them in place. Thus the leaves became flat at first, and have so remained through all the days of mankind. The plants lifted the sky inch by inch until men were able to crawl about between the heavens and the earth, and thus pass from place to place and visit one another.

After a long time, according to the Hawaiian legends, a man, supposed to be Maui, came to a woman and said: "Give me a drink from your gourd calabash, and I will push the heavens higher." The woman handed the gourd to him. When he had taken a deep draught, he braced himself against the clouds and lifted them to the height of the trees. Again he hoisted the sky and carried it to the tops of the mountains; then with great exertion he thrust it upwards once more, and pressed it to the place it now occupies. Nevertheless dark clouds many times hang low along the eastern slope of Maui's great mountain—Haleakala—and descend in heavy rains upon the hill Kauwiki; but they dare not stay, lest Maui the strong come and hurl them so far away that they cannot come back again.

A man who had been watching the process of lifting the sky ridiculed Maui for attempting such a difficult task. When the clouds rested on the tops of the mountains, Maui turned to punish his critic. The man had fled to the other side of the island, Maui rapidly pursued and finally caught him on the sea coast, not many miles north of the town now known as Lahaina. After a brief struggle the man was changed, according to the story, into a great black rock, which can be seen by any traveler who desires to localize the legends of Hawaii.

In Samoa Tiitii, the latter part of the full name of Mauikiikii, is used as the name of the one who braced his feet against the rocks and pushed the sky up. The foot-prints, some six feet long, are said to be shown by the natives.

Another Samoan story is almost like the raw Hawaiian legend. The heavens had fallen, people crawled, but the leaves pushed up a little; but the sky was uneven. Men tried to walk, but hit their heads, and in this confined space it was very hot. A woman rewarded a man who lifted the sky to its proper place by giving him a drink of water from her cocoanut shell.

A number of small groups of islands in the Pacific have legends of their skies being lifted, but they attribute the labor to the great eels and serpents of the sea.

One of the Ellice group, Niu Island, says that as the serpent began to lift the sky the people clapped their hands and shouted "Lift up!" "High!" "Higher!" But the body of the serpent finally broke into pieces which became islands, and the blood sprinkled its drops on the sky and became stars.

One of the Samoan legends says that a plant called daiga, which had one large umbrella-like leaf, pushed up the sky and gave it its shape.

The Vatupu, or Tracey Islanders, said at one time the sky and rocks were united. Then steam or clouds of smoke rose from the rocks, and, pouring out in volumes, forced the sky away from the earth. Man appeared in these clouds of steam or smoke. Perspiration burst forth as this man forced his way through the heated atmosphere. From this perspiration woman was formed. Then were born three sons, two of whom pushed up the sky. One, in the north, pushed as far as his arms would reach. The one in the south was short and climbed a hill, pushing as he went up, until the sky was in its proper place.

The Gilbert Islanders say the sky was pushed up by men with long poles.

The ancient New Zealanders understood incantations by which they could draw up or discover. They found a land where the sky and the earth were united. They prayed over their stone axe and cut the sky and land apart. "Hau-hau-tu" was the name of the great stone axe by which the sinews of the great heaven above were severed, and Langi (sky) was separated from, Papa (earth).

The New Zealand Maoris were accustomed to say that at first the sky rested close upon the earth and therefore there was utter darkness for ages. Then the six sons of heaven and earth, born during this period of darkness, felt the need of light and discussed the necessity of separating their parents-the sky from the earth-and decided to attempt the work.

Rongo (Hawaiian god Lono) the "father of food plants," attempted to lift the sky, but could not tear it from the earth. Then Tangaroa (Kanaloa), the "father of fish and reptiles," failed. Haumia Tiki-tiki (Maui Kiikii), the "father of wild food plants," could not raise the clouds. Then Tu (Hawaiian Ku), the "father of fierce men," struggled in vain, But Tane (Hawaiian Kane), the "father of giant forests," pushed and lifted until he thrust the sky far up above him. Then they discovered their descendants-the multitude of human beings who had been living on the earth concealed and crushed by the clouds. Afterwards the last son, Tawhiri (father of storms), was angry and waged war against his brothers. He hid in the sheltered hollows of the great skies. There he begot his vast brood of winds and storms with which he finally drove all his brothers and their descendants into hiding places on land and sea. The New Zealanders mention the names of the canoes in which their ancestors fled from the old home Hawaiki.

Tu (father of fierce men) and his descendants, however, conquered wind and storm and have ever since held supremacy.

The New Zealand legends also say that heaven and earth have never lost their love for each other. "The warm sighs of earth ever ascend from the wooded mountains and valleys, and men call them mists. The sky also lets fall frequent tears which men term dew drops."

The Manihiki islanders say that Maui desired to separate the sky from the earth. His father, Ru, was the supporter of the heavens. Maui persuaded him to assist in lifting the burden. Maui went to the north and crept into a place, where, lying prostrate under the sky, he could brace himself against it and push with great power. in the same way Ru went to the south and braced himself against the southern skies. Then they made the signal, and both pressed "with their backs against the solid blue mass." It gave way before the great strength of the father and son. Then they lifted again, bracing themselves with hands and knees against the earth. They crowded it and bent it upward. They were able to stand with the sky resting on their shoulders. They heaved against the bending mass, and it receded rapidly. They quickly put the palms of their hands under it; then the tips of their fingers, and it retreated farther and farther. At last, "drawing themselves out to gigantic proportions, they pushed the entire heavens up to the very lofty position which they have ever since occupied."

But Maui and Ru had not worked perfectly together; therefore the sky was twisted and its surface was very irregular. They determined to smooth the sky before they finished their task, so they took large stone adzes and chipped off the rough protuberances and ridges, until by and by the great arch was cut out and smoothed off. They then took finer tools and chipped and polished until the sky became the beautifully finished blue dome which now bends around the earth.

The Hervey island myth, as related by W. W. Gill, states that Ru, the father of Maui, came from Avaiki (Hawa-iki), the underworld or abode of the spirits of the dead. He found men crowded down by the sky, which was a mass of solid blue stone. He was very sorry when he saw the condition of the inhabitants of the earth, and planned to raise the sky a little. So he planted stakes of different kinds of trees. These were strong enough to hold the sky so far above the earth "that men could stand erect and walk about without inconvenience." This was celebrated in one of the Hervey Island songs:

"Force up the heavens,
O, Ru!
And let the space be clear."

For this helpful deed Ru received the name "The supporter of the heavens." He was rather proud of his achievement and was gratified because of the praise received. So he came sometimes and looked at the stakes and the beautiful blue sky resting on them. Maui, the son, came along and ridiculed his father for thinking so much of his work. Maui is not represented, in the legends, as possessing a great deal of love and reverence for his relatives provided his affection interfered with his mischief; so it was not at all strange that he laughed at his father. Ru became angry and said to Maui: "Who told youngsters to talk? Take care of yourself, or I will hurl you out of existence."

Maui dared him to try it. Ru quickly seized him and "threw him to a great height." But Maui changed himself to a bird and sank back to earth unharmed.

Then he changed himself back into the form of a man, and, making himself very large, ran and thrust his head between the old man's legs. He pried and lifted until Ru and the sky around him began to give. Another lift and he hurled them both to such a height that the sky could not come back.

Ru himself was entangled among the stars. His head and shoulders stuck fast, and he could not free himself. How he struggled, until the skies shook, while Maui went away. Maui was proud of his achievement in having moved the sky so far away. In this self-rejoicing he quickly forgot his father.

Ru died after a time. "His body rotted away and his bones, of vast proportions, came tumbling down from time to time, and were shivered on the earth into countless fragments. These shattered bones of Ru are scattered over every hill and valley of one of the islands, to the very edge of the sea."

Thus the natives of the Hervey Islands account for the many pieces of porous lava and the small pieces of pumice stone found occasionally in their islands. The "bones" were very light and greatly resembled fragments of real bone. If the fragments were large enough they were sometimes taken and worshiped as gods. One of these pieces, of extraordinary size, was given to Mr. Gill when the natives were bringing in a large collection of idols. "This one was known as 'The Light Stone,' and was worshiped as the god of the wind and the waves. Upon occasions of a hurricane, incantations and offerings of food would be made to it."

Thus, according to different Polynesian legends, Maui raised the sky and made the earth inhabitable for his fellow-men.

IV

Maui Snaring the Sun

"Maui became restless and fought the sun
With a noose that he laid.
And winter won the sun,
And summer was won by Maui."

—Queen Liliuokalani's family chant

A very unique legend is found among the widely-scattered Polynesians. The story of Maui's "Snaring the Sun" was told among the Maoris of New Zealand, the Kanakas of the Hervey and Society Islands, and the ancient natives of Hawaii. The Samoans tell the same story without mentioning the name of Maui. They say that the snare was cast by a child of the sun itself.

The Polynesian stories of the origin of the sun are worthy of note before the le end of the change from short to long days is given.

The Tongan Islanders, according to W. W. Gill, tell the story of the origin of the sun and moon. They say that Vatea (Wakea) and their ancestor Tongaiti quarreled concerning a child—each claiming it as his own. In the struggle the child was cut in two. Vatea squeezed and rolled the part he secured into a ball and threw it away, far up into the heavens, where it became the sun. It shone brightly as it rolled along the heavens, and sank down to Avaiki (Hawaii), the nether world. But the ball came back again and once more rolled across the sky. Tonga-iti had let his half of the child fall on the ground and lie there, until made envious by the beautiful ball Vatea made.

At last he took the flesh which lay on the ground and made it into a ball. As the sun sank he threw his ball up into the darkness, and it rolled along the heavens, but the blood had drained out of the flesh while it lay upon the ground, therefore it could not become so red and burning as the sun, and had not life to move so swiftly. It was as white as a dead body, because its blood was all gone; and it could not make the darkness flee away as the sun had done. Thus day and night and the sun and moon always remain with the earth.

The legends of the Society Islands say that a demon in the west became angry with the sun and in his rage ate it up, causing night. In the same way a demon from the east would devour the moon, but for some reason these angry ones could not destroy their captives and were compelled to open their mouths and let the bright balls come forth once more. In some places a sacrifice of some one of distinction was needed to placate the wrath of the devourers and free the balls of light in times of eclipse.

The moon, pale and dead in appearance, moved slowly; while the sun, full of life and strength, moved quickly. Thus days were very short and nights were very long. Mankind suffered from the fierceness of the heat of the sun and also from its prolonged absence. Day and night were alike a burden to men. The darkness was so great and lasted so long that fruits would not ripen.

After Maui had succeeded in throwing the heavens into their place, and fastening them so that they could not fall, he learned that he had opened a way for the sun-god to come up from the lower world and rapidly run across the blue vault. This made two troubles for men-the heat of the sun was very great and the journey too quickly over. Maui planned to capture the sun and punish him for thinking so little about the welfare of mankind.

As Rev. A. O. Forbes, a missionary among the Hawaiians, relates, Maui's mother was troubled very much by the heedless haste of the sun. She had many kapa-cloths to make, for this was the only kind of clothing known in Hawaii, except sometimes a woven mat or a long grass fringe worn as a skirt. This native cloth was made by pounding the fine bark of certain trees with wooden mallets until the fibres were beaten and ground into a wood pulp. Then she pounded the pulp into thin sheets from which the best sleeping mats and clothes could be fashioned. These kapa cloths had to be thoroughly dried, but the days were so short that by the time she had spread out the kapa the sun had heedlessly rushed across the sky and gone down into the under-world, and all the cloth had to be gathered up again and cared for until another day should come. There were other troubles. "The food could not be prepared and cooked in one day. Even an incantation to the gods could not be chanted through ere they were overtaken by darkness."

This was very discouraging and caused great suffering, as well as much unnecessary trouble and labor. Many complaints were made against the thoughtless sun.

Maui pitied his mother and determined to make the sun go slower that the days might be long enough to satisfy the needs of men. Therefore, he went over to the northwest of the island on which he lived. This was Mt. Iao, an extinct volcano, in which lies one of the most beautiful and picturesque valleys of the Hawaiian Islands. He climbed the ridges until he could see the course of the sun as it passed over the island. He saw that the sun came up the eastern side of Mt. Haleakala. He crossed over the plain between the two mountains and climbed to the top of Mt. Haleakala. There he watched the burning sun as it came up from Koolau and passed directly over the top of the mountain. The summit of Haleakala is a great extinct crater twenty miles in circumference, and nearly twenty-five hundred feet in depth. There are two tremendous gaps or chasms in the side of the crater wall, through which in days gone by the massive bowl poured forth its flowing lava. One of these was the Koolau, or eastern gap, in which Maui probably planned to catch the sun.

Mt. Hale-a-ka-la of the Hawaiian Islands means House-of-the-sun. "La," or "Ra," is the name of the sun throughout parts of Polynesia. Ra was the sun-god of ancient Egypt. Thus the antiquities of Polynesia and Egypt touch each other, and today no man knows the full reason thereof.

The Hawaiian legend says Maui was taunted by a man who ridiculed the idea that he could snare the sun, saying, "You will never catch the sun. You are only an idle nobody."

Maui replied, "When I conquer my enemy and my desire is attained, I will be your death."

After studying the path of the sun, Maui returned to his mother and told her that he would go and cut off the legs of the sun so that he could not run so fast.

His mother said: "Are you strong enough for this work?" He said, 'Yes." Then she gave him fifteen strands of well-twisted fiber and told him to go to his grandmother, who lived in the great crater of Haleakala, for the rest of the things in his conflict with the sun. She said: "You must climb the mountain to the place where a large wiliwili tree is standing. There you will find the place where the sun stops to eat cooked bananas prepared by your grandmother.

Stay there until a rooster crows three times; then watch your grandmother go out to make a fire and put on food. You had better take her bananas. She will look for them and find you and ask who you are. Tell her you belong to Hina."

When she had taught him all these things, he went tip the mountain to Kaupo to the place Hina had directed. There was a large wiliwili tree. Here he waited for the rooster to crow. The name of that rooster was Kalauhele-moa. When the rooster had crowed three times, the grandmother came out with a bunch of bananas to cook for the sun. She took off the upper part of the bunch and laid it down. Maui immediately snatched it away. In a moment she turned to pick it up, but could not find it. She was angry and cried out: "Where are the bananas of the sun?" Then she took off another part of the bunch, and Maui stole that. Thus he did until all the bunch had been taken away. She was almost blind and could not detect him by sight, so she sniffed all around her until she detected the smell of a man. She asked—"Who are you? To whom do you belong?" Maui replied: "I belong to Hina." "Why have you come?" Maui told her, "I have come to kill the sun. He goes so fast that he never dries the tapa Hina has beaten out."

The old woman gave a magic stone for a battle axe and one more rope. She taught him how to catch the sun, saying: "Make a place to hide here by this large wiliwili tree. When the first leg of the sun comes up, catch it with your first rope, and so on until you have used all your ropes. Fasten them to the tree, then take the stone axe to strike the body of the sun."

Maui dug a hole among the roots of the tree and concealed himself. Soon the first ray of light—the first leg of the sun—came up along the mountain side. Maui threw his rope and caught it. One by one the legs of the sun came over the edge of the crater's rim and were caught. Only one long leg was still hanging down the side of the mountain. It was hard for the sun to move that leg. It shook and trembled and tried hard to come up. At last it crept over the edge and was caught by Maui with the rope given by his grandmother.

When the sun saw that his sixteen long legs were held fast in the ropes, he began to go back down the mountain side into the sea. Then Maui tied the ropes fast to the tree and pulled until the body of the sun came up again. Brave Maui caught his magic stone club or axe, and began to strike and wound the sun, until he cried: "Give me my life." Maui said: "If you live, you may be a traitor. Perhaps I had better kill you." But the sun begged for life. After they had conversed a while, they agreed that there should be a regular motion in the journey of the sun. There should be longer days, and. yet half the time he might go quickly as in the winter time, but the other half he must move slowly as in summer. Thus men dwelling on the earth should be blessed.

Another legend says that he made a lasso and climbed to the summit of Mt. Haleakala. He made ready his lasso, so that when the sun came lip the mountain side and rose above him he could cast the noose and catch the sun, but he only snared one of the sun's larger rays and broke it off. Again and again he threw the lasso until he had broken off all the strong rays of the sun.

Then he shouted exultantly, "Thou art my captive; I will kill thee for going so swiftly."

Then the sun said, "Let me live and thou shalt see me go more slowly hereafter. Behold, hast thou not broken off all my strong legs and left me only the weak ones?"

So the agreement was made, and Maui permitted the sun to pursue his course, and from that day he went more slowly.

Maui returned from his conflict with the sun and sought for Moemoe, the man who had ridiculed him. Maui chased this man around the island from one side to the other until they had passed through Lahaina (one of the first mission stations in 1828). There on the seashore near the large black rock of the legend of Maui lifting the sky he found Moemoe. Then they left the seashore and the contest raged up hill and down until Maui slew the man and "changed the body into a long rock, which is there to this day, by the side of the road going past Black Rock."

Before the battle with the sun occurred Maui went down into the underworld, according to the New Zealand tradition, and remained a long time with his relatives. In some way he learned that there was an enchanted jawbone in the possession of some one of his ancestors, so he waited and waited, hoping that at last he might discover it.

After a time he noticed that presents of food were being sent away to some person whom he had not met.

One day he asked the messengers, "Who is it you are taking that present of food to?"

The people answered, "It is for Muri, your ancestress."

Then he asked for the food, saying, "I will carry it to her myself."

But he took the food away and hid it. "And this he did for many days," and the presents failed to reach the old woman.

By and by she suspected mischief, for it did not seem as if her friends would neglect her so long a time, so she thought she would catch the tricky one and eat him. She depended upon her sense of smell to detect the one who had troubled her. As Sir George Grey tells the story: "When Maui came along the path carrying the present of food, the old chiefess sniffed and sniffed until she was sure that she smelt some one coming. She was very much exasperated, and her stomach began to distend itself that she might be ready to devour this one when he came near.

Then she turned toward the south and sniffed. and not a scent of anything reached her. Then she turned to the north, and to the cast, but could not detect the odor of a human being. She made one more trial and turned toward the west. Ah! then came the scent of a man to her plainly and she called out, 'I know, from the smell wafted to me by the breeze, that somebody is close to me.'"

Maui made known his presence and the old woman knew that he was a descendant of hers, and her stomach began immediately to shrink and contract itself again.

Then she asked, "Art thou Maui?"

He answered, "Even so," and told her that he wanted "the jaw-bone by which great enchantments could be wrought."

Then Muri, the old chiefess, gave him the magic bone and he returned to his brothers, who were still living on the earth.

Then Maui said: "Let us now catch the sun in a noose that we may compel him to move more slowly in order that mankind may have long days to labor in and procure subsistence for themselves."

They replied, "No man can approach it on account of the fierceness of the heat."

According to the Society Island legend, his mother advised him to have nothing to do with the sun, who was a divine living creature, "in form like a man, possessed of fearful energy," shaking his golden locks both morning and evening in the eyes of men. Many persons had tried to regulate the movements of the sun, but had failed completely.

But Maui encouraged his mother and his brothers by asking them to remember his power to protect himself by the use of enchantments.

The Hawaiian legend says that Maui himself gathered cocoanut fibre in great quantity and manufactured it into strong ropes. But the legends of other islands say that he had the aid of his brothers, and while working learned many useful lessons. While winding and twisting they discovered how to make square ropes and flat ropes as well as the ordinary round rope. In the Society Islands, it is said, Maui and his brothers made six strong ropes of great length. These he called aeiariki (royal nooses).

The New Zealand legend says that when Maui and his brothers had finished making all the ropes required they took provisions and other things needed and journeyed toward the east to find the place where the sun should rise. Maui carried with him the magic jaw-bone which he had secured from Muri, his ancestress, in the under-world.

They traveled all night and concealed themselves by day so that the sun should not see them and become too suspicious and watchful. In this way they journeyed, until "at length they had gone very far to the eastward and had come to the very edge of the place out of which the sun rises. There they set to work and built on each side a long, high wall of clay, with hilts of boughs of trees at each end to hide themselves in."

Here they laid a large noose made from their ropes and Maui concealed himself on one side of this place along which the sun must come, while his brothers hid on the other side.

Maui seized his magic enchanted jaw-bone as the weapon with which to fight the sun, and ordered his brothers to pull hard on the noose and not to be frightened or moved to set the sun free.

"At last the sun came rising up out of his place like a fire spreading far and wide over the mountains and forests.

He rises up.

His head passes through the noose.

The ropes are pulled tight.

Then the monster began to struggle and roll himself about, while the snare jerked backwards and forwards as he struggled. Ah! was not he held fast in the ropes of his enemies.

Then forth rushed that bold hero Maui with his enchanted weapon. The sun screamed aloud and roared. Maui struck him fiercely with many blows. They held him for a long time. At last they let him go, and then weak from wounds the sun crept very slowly and feebly along his course."

In this way the days were made longer so that men could perform their daily tasks and fruits and food plants could have time to grow.

The legend of the Hervey group of islands says that Maui made six snares and placed them at intervals along the path over which the sun must pass. The sun in the form of a man climbed up from Avaiki (Hawaiki). Maui pulled the first noose, but it slipped down the rising sun until it caught and was pulled tight around his feet.

Maui ran quickly to pull the ropes of the second snare, but that also slipped down, down, until it was tightened around the knees. Then Maui hastened to the third snare, while the sun was trying to rush along on his journey. The third snare caught around the hips. The fourth snare fastened itself around the waist. The fifth slipped under the arms, and yet the sun sped along as if but little inconvenienced by Maui's efforts.

Then Maui caught the last noose and threw it around the neck of the sun, and fastened the rope to a spur of rock. The sun struggled until nearly strangled to death and then gave up, promising Maui that he would go as slowly as was desired. Maui left the snares fastened to the sun to keep him in constant fear.

"These ropes may still be seen hanging from the sun at dawn and stretching into the skies when he descends into the ocean at night. By the assistance of these ropes he is gently let down into Ava-iki in the evening, and also raised up out of shadow-land in the morning."

Another legend from the Society Islands is related by Mr. Gill:

Maui tried many snares before he could catch the sun. The sun was the Hercules, or the Samson, of the heavens. He broke the strong cords of cocoanut fibre which Maui made and placed around the opening by which the sun climbed out from the under-world. Maui made stronger ropes, but still the sun broke them every one.

Then Maui thought of his sister's hair, the sister Inaika, whom he cruelly treated in later years. Her hair was long and beautiful. He cut off some of it and made a strong rope. With this he lassoed or rather snared the sun, and caught him around the throat. The sun quickly promised to be more thoughtful of the needs of men and go at a more reasonable pace across the sky.

A story from the American Indians is told in Hawaii's Young People, which is very similar to the Polynesian legends.

An Indian boy became very angry with the sun for getting so warm and making his clothes shrink with the heat. He told his sister to make a snare. The girl took sinews from a large deer, but they shriveled under the heat. She took her own long hair and made snares, but they were burned in a moment. Then she tried the fibres of various plants and was successful. Her brother took the fibre cord and drew it through his lips. It stretched and became a strong red cord. He pulled and it became very long. He went to the place of sunrise, fixed his snare, and caught the sun. When the sun had been sufficiently punished, the animals of the earth studied the problem of setting the sun free. At last a mouse as large as a mountain ran and gnawed the red cord. It broke and the sun moved on, but the poor mouse had been burned and shriveled into the small mouse of the present day.

A Samoan legend says that a woman living for a tinie with the sun bore a child who had the name "Child of the Sun." She wanted gifts for the child's marriage, so she took a long vine, climbed a tree, made the vine into a noose, lassoed the sun, and made him give her a basket of blessings.

In Fiji, the natives tie the grasses growing on a hilltop over which they are passing, when traveling from place to place. They do this to make a snare to catch the sun if he should try to go down before they reach the end of their day's journey.

This legend is a misty memory of some time when the Polynesian people were in contact with the short days of the extreme north or south. It is a very remarkable exposition of a fact of nature perpetuated many centuries in lands absolutely free from such natural phenomena.

V

Maui Finding Fire

"Grant, oh grant me thy hidden fire,
O Banyan Tree.
Perform an incantation,
Utter a prayer
To the Banyan Tree.
Kindle a fire in the dust
Of the Banyan Tree."

—Translation of ancient Polynesian chant

Among students of mythology certain characters in the legends of the various nations are known as "culture heroes." Mankind has from time to time learned exceedingly useful lessons and has also usually ascribed the new knowledge to some noted person in the national mythology. These mythical benefactors who have brought these practical benefits to men are placed among the "hero gods." They have been teachers or "culture heroes" to mankind.

Probably the fire finders of the different nations are among the best remembered of all these benefactors. This would naturally be the case, for no greater good has touched man's physical life than the discovery of methods of making fire.

Prometheus, the classical fire finder, is most widely known in literature. But of all the helpful gods of mythology, Maui, the mischievous Polynesian, is beyond question the hero of the largest numbers of nations scattered over the widest extent of territory. Prometheus belonged to Rome, but Maui belonged to the length and breadth of the Pacific Ocean. Theft or trickery, the use of deceit of some kind, is almost inseparably connected with fire finding all over the world. Prometheus stole fire from, Jupiter and gave it to men together with the genius to make use of it in the arts and sciences. He found the rolling chariot of the sun, secretly filled his hollow staff with fire, carried it to earth, put a part in the breast of man to create enthusiasm or animation, and saved the remainder for the comfort of mankind to be used with the artist skill of Minerva and Vulcan. In Brittany the golden or fire-crested wren steals fire and is red-marked while so doing. The animals of the North American Indians are represented as stealing fire sometimes from the cuttle fish and sometimes from one another. Some swiftly-flying bird or fleet-footed coyote would carry the stolen fire to the home of the tribe.

The possession of fire meant to the ancients all that wealth means family of today. It meant the possession of comfort. The gods were naturally determined to keep this wealth in their own hands. For any one to make a sharp deal and cheat a god of fire out of a part of this valuable property or to make a courageous raid upon the fire guardian and steal the treasure, was easily sufficient to make that one a "culture hero." As a matter of fact a prehistoric family without fire would go to any length in order to get it. The fire finders would naturally be the hero-gods and stealing fire would be an exploit rather than a crime.

It is worth noting that in many myths not only was fire stolen, but birds marked by red or black spots among their feathers were associated with the theft. It would naturally be supposed that the Hawaiians living in a volcanic country with ever-flowing fountains of lava, would connect their fire myths with some volcano when relating the story of the origin of fire. But like the rest of the Polynesians, they found fire in trees rather than in rivers of melted rock. They must have brought their fire legends and fire customs with them when they came to the islands of active volcanoes.

Flint rocks as fire producers are not found in the Hawaiian myths, nor in the stories from the island groups related to the Hawaiians. Indians might see the fleeing buffalo strike fire from the stones under his hard hoofs. The Tartars might have a god to teach them "the secret of the stone's edge and the iron's hardness." The Peruvians could very easily form a legend of their mythical father Guamansuri finding a way to make fire after he had seen the sling stones, thrown at his enemies, bring forth sparks of fire from the rocks against which they struck. The thunder and the lightning of later years were the sparks and the crash of stones hurled among the cloud mountains by the mighty gods.

In Australia the story is told of an old man and his daughter who lived in great darkness. After a time the father found the doorway of light through which the sun passed on his journey. He opened the door and a flood of sunshine covered the earth. His daughter looked around her home and saw numbers of serpents. She seized a staff and began to kill them. She wielded it so vigorously that it became hot in her bands.

At last it broke, but the pieces rubbed against each other and flashed into sparks and flames. Thus it was learned that fire was buried in wood.

Flints were known in Europe and Asia and America, but the Polynesian looked to the banyan and kindred trees for the hidden sparks of fire. The natives of De Peyster's Island say that their ancestors learned how to make fire by seeing smoke rise from crossed branches rubbing together while trees were shaken by fierce winds.

In studying the Maui myths of the Pacific it is necessary to remember that Polynesians use "t" and "k" without distinguishing them apart, and also as in the Hawaiian Islands an apostrophe (') is often used in place of "t" or "k". Therefore the Maui Ki-i-k-i'i of Hawaii becomes the demi-god Tiki-tiki of the Gilbert Islands-or the Ti'i-ti'i of Samoa or the Tiki of New Zealand-or other islands of the great ocean. We must also remember that in the Hawaiian legends Kalana is Maui's father. This in other groups becomes Talanga or Kalanga or Karanga. Kanaloa, the great god of most of the different Polynesians, is also sometimes called the Father of Maui. It is not strange that some of the exploits usually ascribed to Maui should be in some places transferred to his father under one name or the other. On one or two groups Mafuia, an ancestress of Maui, is mentioned as finding the fire. The usual legend makes Maui the one who takes fire away from Mafuia. The story of fire finding in Polynesia sifts itself to Maui under one of his widely-accepted names, or to his father or to his ancestress-with but very few exceptions. This fact is important as showing in a very marked manner the race relationship of a vast number of the islanders of the Pacific world. From the Marshall Islands, in the west, to the Society Islands of the east; from the Hawaiian Islands in the north to the New Zealand group in the south, the footsteps of the fire finder can be traced.

The Hawaiian story of fire finding is one of the least marvelous of all the legends. Hina, Maui's mother, wanted fish. One morning early Maui saw that the great storm waves of the sea had died down and the fishing grounds could be easily reached. He awakened his brothers and with them hastened to the beach. This was at Kaupo on the island of Maui. Out into the gray shadows of the dawn they paddled.

When they were far from shore they began to fish. But Maui, looking landward, saw a fire on the mountain side.

"Behold," he cried. "There is a fire burning. Whose can this fire be?"

"Whose, indeed?" his brothers replied.

"Let us hasten to the shore and cook our food," said one.

They decided that they had better catch some fish to cook before they returned. Thus, in the morning, before the hot sun drove the fish deep down to the dark recesses of the sea, they fished until a bountiful supply lay in the bottom of the canoe.

When they came to land, Maui leaped out and ran up the mountain side to get the fire. For a long, long time they had been without fire. The great volcano Haleakala above then, had become extinct—and they had lost the coals they had tried to keep alive. They had eaten fruits and uncooked roots and the shell fish broken from the reef—and sometimes the great raw fish from the far-out ocean. But now they hoped to gain living fire and cooked food.

But when Maui rushed up toward the cloudy pillar of smoke he saw a family of birds scratching the fire out. Their work was finished and they flew away just as he reached the place.

Maui and his brothers watched for fire day after day—but the birds, the curly-tailed Alae (or the mudhens) made no fire. Finally the brothers went fishing once more—but when they looked toward the mountain, again they saw flames and smoke. Thus it happened to them again and again.

Maui proposed to his brothers that they go fishing leaving him to watch the birds. But the Alae counted the fishermen and refused to build a fire for the hidden one who was watching them. They said among themselves, "Three are in the boat and we know not where the other one is, we will make no fire today."

So the experiment failed again and again. If one or two remained or if all waited on the land there would be no fire—but the dawn which saw the four brothers in the boat, saw also the fire on the land.

Finally Maui rolled some kapa cloth together and stuck it up in one end of the canoe so that it would look like a man. He then concealed himself near the haunt of the mud-hens, while his brothers went out fishing. The birds counted the figures in the boat and then started to build a heap of wood for the fire.

Maui was impatient—and just as the old Alae began to select sticks with which to make the flames he leaped swiftly out and caught her and held her prisoner. He forgot for a moment that he wanted the secret of fire making. In his anger against the wise bird his first impulse was to taunt her and then kill her for hiding the secret of fire.

But the Alae cried out: "If you are the death of me—my secret will perish also—and you cannot have fire."

Maui then promised to spare her life if she would tell him what to do.

Then came the contest of wits. The bird told the demi-god to rub the stalks of water plants together. He guarded the bird and tried the plants. Water instead of fire ran out of the twisted stems. Then she told him to rub reeds together—but they bent and broke and could make no fire. He twisted her neck until she was half dead-then she cried out: "I have hidden the fire in a green stick."

Maui worked hard, but not a spark of fire appeared. Again he caught his prisoner by the head and wrung her neck, and she named a kind of dry wood. Maui rubbed the sticks together, but they only became warm. The neck twisting process was resumed and repeated again and again, until the mud-hen was almost dead-and Maui had tried tree after tree. At last Maui found fire. Then as the flames rose he said: "There is one more thing to rub." He took a fire stick and rubbed the top of the head of his prisoner until the feathers fell off and the raw flesh appeared. Thus the Hawaiian mud-hen and her descendants have ever since had bald heads, and the Hawaiians have had the secret of fire making.

Another Hawaiian legend places the scene of Maui's contest with the mud-hens a little inland of the town of Hilo on the Island of Hawaii. There are three small extinct craters very near each other known as The Halae Hills. One, the southern or Puna side of the hills, is a place called Pohaku-nui. Here dwelt two brother birds of the Alae family. They were gods. One had the power of fire making. Here at Pohaku-nui they were accustomed to kindle a fire and bake their dearly loved food-baked bananas. Here Maui planned to learn the secret of fire. The birds had kindled the fire and the bananas were almost done, when the elder Alae called to the younger: "Be quick, here comes the swift son of Hina."

The birds scratched out the fire, caught the bananas and fled. Maui told his mother he would follow them until he learned the secret of fire. His mother encouraged him because he was very strong and very swift. So he followed the birds from place to place as they fled from him, finding new spots on which to make their fires. At last they came to the island Oahu. There he saw a great fire and a multitude of birds gathered around it, chattering loudly and trying to hasten the baking of the bananas. Their incantation was this: "Let us cook quick." "Let us cook quick." "The swift child of Hina will come."

Maui's mother Hina had taught him how to know the fire-maker. "If you go up to the fire, you will find many birds. Only one is the guardian. This is the small, young Alae. His name is Alae-iki: Only this one knows how to make fire." So whenever Maui came near to the fire-makers he always sought for the little Alae. Sometimes he made mistakes and soirietimes almost captured the one he desired. At Waianae he leaped suddenly among the birds. They scattered the fire, and the younger bird tried to snatch his banana from the coals and flee, but Maui seized him and began to twist his neck. The bird cried out, warning Maui not to kill him or he would lose the secret of fire altogether. Maui was told that the fire was made from a banana stump. He saw the bananas roasting and thought this was reasonable. So, according to directions, he began to rub together pieces of the banana. The bird hoped for an unguarded moment when be might escape, but Maui was very watchful and was also very angry when he found that rubbing only resulted in squeezing out juice. Then he twisted the neck of the bird and was told to rub the stem of the taro plant. This also was so green that it only produced water. Then he was so angry that he nearly rubbed the head of the bird off-and the bird, fearing for its life, told the truth and taught Maui how to find the wood in which fire dwelt.

They learned to draw out the sparks secreted in different kinds of trees. The sweet sandalwood was one of these fire trees. Its Hawaiian name is "Ili-ahi"—the "ili" (bark) and "ahi" (fire), the bark in which fire is concealed.

A legend of the Society Islands is somewhat similar. Ina (Hina) promised to aid Maui in finding fire for the islanders. She sent him into the under-world to find Tangaroa (Kanaloa). This god Tangaroa held fire in his possession—Maui was to know him by his tattooed face. Down the dark path through the long eaves Maui trod swiftly until he found the god. Maui asked him for fire to take up to men. The god gave him a lighted stick and sent him away. But Maui put the fire out and went back again after fire. This he did several times, until the wearied giver decided to teach the intruder the art of fire making. He called a white duck to aid him. Then, taking two sticks of dry wood, he gave the under one to the bird and rapidly moved the upper stick across the under until fire came, Maui seized the upper stick, after it had been charred in the flame, and burned the head of the bird back of each eye. Thus were made the black spots which mark the head of the white duck. Then arose a quarrel between Tangaroa and Maui—but Maui struck down the god, and, thinking he had killed him, carried away the art of making fire. His father and mother made inquiries about their relative-Maui hastened back to the fire fountain and made the spirit return to the body-then, coming back to Ina, he bade her good bye and carried the fire sticks to the upper-world. The Hawaiians, and probably others among the Polynesians, felt that any state of unconsciousness was a form of death in which the spirit left the body, but was called back by prayers and incantations. Therefore, when Maui restored the god to consciousness, he was supposed to have made the spirit released by death return into the body and bring it back to life.

In the Samoan legends as related by G. Turner, the name Ti'iti'i is used. This is the same as the second name found in Maui Ki'i-ki'i. The Samoan legend of Ti'iti'i is almost identical with the New Zealand fire myth of Maui, and is very similar to the story coming from the Hervey Islands from Savage Island and also from the Tokelau and other island groups. The Samoan story says that the home of Mafuie the earthquake god was in the land of perpetual fire. Maui's or Ti'iti'i's father Talanga (Kalana) was also a resident of the under-world and a great friend of the earthquake god.

Ti'iti'i watched his father as he left his home in the upper-world. Talanga approached a perpendicular wall of rock, said some prayer or incantation—and passed through a door which immediately closed after him. (This is a very near approach to the "open sesame" of the Arabian Nights stories.)

Ti'iti'i went to the rock, but could not find the way through. He determined to conceal himself the next time so near that he could hear his father's words.

After some days he was able to catch all the words uttered by his father as he knocked on the stone door—

"O rock! divide.
I am Talanga,
I come to work
On my land
Given by Mafuie."

Ti'iti'i went to the perpendicular wall and imitating his father's voice called for a rock to open. Down through a cave he passed until he found his father working in the under-world.

The astonished father, learning how his son came, bade him keep very quiet and work lest he arouse the anger of Mafuie. So for a time the boy labored obediently by his father's side.

In a little while the boy saw smoke and asked what it was. The father told him that it was the smoke from the fire of Mafuie, and explained what fire would do.

The boy determined to get some fire—he went to the place from which the smoke arose and there found the god, and asked him for fire. Mafuie gave him fire to carry to his father. The boy quickly had an oven prepared and the fire placed in it to cook some of the taro they had been cultivating. Just as everything was ready an earthquake god came up and blew the fire out and scattered the stones of the oven.

Then Ti'iti'i was angry and began to talk to Mafuie. The god attacked the boy, intending to punish him severely for daring to rebel against the destruction of the fire.

What a battle there was for a time in the underworld! At last Ti'iti'i seized one of the arms of Mafuie and broke it off. He caught the other arm and began to twist and bend it.

Mafuie begged the boy to spare him. His right arm was gone. How could he govern the earthquakes if his left arm were torn off also? It was his duty to hold Samoa level and not permit too many earthquakes. It would be hard to do that even with one arm-but it would be impossible if both arms were gone.

Ti'iti'i listened to the plea and demanded a reward if he should spare the left arm. Alafuie offered Ti'iti'i one hundred wives. The boy did not want them.

Then the god offered to teach him the secret of fire finding to take to the upper-world.

The boy agreed to accept the fire secret, and thus learned that the gods in making the earth had concealed fire in various trees for men to discover in their own good time, and that this fire could be brought out by rubbing pieces of wood together.

The people of Samoa have not had much faith in Mafuie's plea that he needed his left arm in order to keep Samoa level. They say that Mafuie has a long stick or handle to the world under the islands—and when he is angry or wishes to frighten them he moves this handle and easily shakes the islands. When an earthquake comes, they give thanks to Ti'iti'i for breaking off one arm—because if the god had two arms they believe he would shake them unmercifully.

One legend of the Hervey Islands says that Maui and his brothers had been living on uncooked food—but learned that their mother sometimes had delicious food which had been cooked. They learned also that fire was needed in order to cook their food. Then Alatii wanted fire and watched his mother.

Maui's mother was the guardian of the way to the invisible world. When she desired to pass from her home to the other world, she would open a black rock and pass inside. Thus she went to Hawaiki, the underworld. Maui planned to follow her, but first studied the forms of birds that he might assume the body of the strongest and most enduring. After a time he took the shape of a pigeon and, flying to the black rock, passed through the door and flew down the long dark passage-way.

After a time he found the god of fire living in a bunch of banyan sticks. He changed himself into the form of a man and demanded the secret of fire.

The fire god agreed to give Maui fire if he would permit himself to be tossed into the sky by the god's strong arms.

Maui agreed on condition that he should have the right to toss the fire god afterwards.

The fire-god felt certain that there would be only one exercise of strength—he felt that he had everything in his own hands—so readily agreed to the tossing contest. It was his intention to throw his opponent so high that when he fell, if he ever did fall, there would be no antagonist uncrushed.

He seized Maui in his strong arms and, swinging him back and forth, flung him upward-but the moment Maui left his hands he changed himself into a feather and floated softly to the ground.

Then the boy ran swiftly to the god and seized him by the legs and lifted him up. Then he began to increase in size and strength until he had lifted the fire god very high. Suddenly he tossed the god upward and caught him as he fell—again and again—until the bruised and dizzy god cried enough, and agreed to give the victor whatever he demanded.

Maui asked for the secret of fire producing. The god taught him how to rub the dry sticks of certain kinds of trees together, and, by friction, produce fire, and especially how fire could be produced by rubbing fire sticks in the fine dust of the banyan tree.

A Society Island legend says Maui borrowed a sacred red pigeon, belonging to one of the gods, and, changing himself into a dragon fly, rode this pigeon through a black rock into Avaiki (Hawaiki), the fire-land of the under-world. He found the god of fire, Mau-ika, living in a house built from a banyan tree. Mau-ika taught Maui the kinds of wood into which when fire went out on the earth a fire goddess had thrown sparks in order to preserve fire. Among these were the "au" (Hawaiian hau), or "the lemon hibiscus"—the "argenta," the "fig" and the "banyan." She taught him also how to make fire by swift motion when rubbing the sticks of these trees. She also gave him coals for his present need.

But Maui was viciously mischievous and set the banyan house on fire, then mounted his pigeon and fled toward the upper-world. But the flames hastened after him and burst out through the rock doors into the sunlit land above—as if it were a volcanic eruption.

The Tokelau Islanders say that Talanga (Kalana) known in other groups of islands as the father of Maui, desired fire in order to secure warmth and cooked food. He went down, down, very far down in the caves of the earth. In the lower world he found Mafuika—an old blind woman, who was the guardian of fire. He told her he wanted fire to take back to men. She refused either to give fire or to teach how to make it. Talanga threatened to kill her, and finally persuaded her to teach how to make fire in any place he might dwell-and the proper trees to use, the fire-yielding trees. She also taught him how to cook food—and also the kind of fish he should cook, and the kinds which should be eaten raw. Thus mankind learned about food as well as fire.

The Savage Island legend adds the element of danger to Maui's mischievous theft of fire. The lad followed his father one day and saw him pull up a bunch of reeds and go down into the fire-land beneath. Maui hastened down to see what his father was doing.

Soon he saw his oportunity to steal the secret of fire. Then he caught some fire and started for the upperworld.

His father caught a glimpse of the young thief and tried to stop him.

Maui ran up the passage through the black cave—bushes and trees bordered his road.

The father hastened after his son and was almost ready to lay hands upon him, when Maui set fire to the bushes. The flames spread rapidly, catching the underbrush and the trees on all sides and burst out in the face of the pursuer. Destruction threatened the under-world, but Maui sped along his way. Then he saw that the fire was chasing him. Bush after bush leaped into flame and hurled sparks and smoke and burning air after him. Choked and smoke-surrounded, he broke through the door of the cavern and found the fresh air of the world. But the flames followed him and swept out in great power upon the upperworld a mighty volcanic eruption.

The New Zealand legends picture Maui as putting out, in one night, all the fires of his people. This was serious mischief, and Maui's mother decided that he should go to the under-world and see his ancestress, Mahuika, the guardian of fire, and get new fire to repair the injury he had wrought. She warned him against attempting to play tricks upon the inhabitants of the lower regions.

Maui gladly hastened down the cave-path to the house of Mahuika, and asked for fire for the upperworld. In some way he pleased her so that she pulled off a finger nail in which fire was burning and gave it to him. As soon as he had gone back to a place where there was water, he put the fire out and returned to Mahuika, asking another gift, which he destroyed. This he did for both hands and feet until only one nail remained. Maui wanted this. Then Mahuika became angry and threw the last finger nail on the ground. Fire poured out and laid hold of everything. Maui ran up the path to the upper-world, but the fire was swifter-footed. Then Maui changed himself into an eagle and flew high up into the air, but the fire and smoke still followed him. Then he saw water and dashed into it, but it was too hot. Around him the forests were blazing, the earth burning and the sea boiling. Maui, about to perish, called on the gods for rain. Then floods of water fell and the fire was checked. The great rain fell on Mahuika and she fled, almost drowned. Her stores of fire were destroyed, quenched by the storm. But in order to save fire for the use of men, as she fled she threw sparks into different kinds of trees where the rain could not reach them, so that when fire was needed it might be brought into the world again by rubbing together the fire sticks.

The Chatham Islanders give the following incantation, which they said was used by Maui against the fierce flood of fire which was pursuing him:

> "To the roaring thunder;
> To the great rain—the long rain;
> To the drizzling rain—the small rain;
> To the rain pattering on the leaves.
> These are the storms—the storms
> Cause them to fall;
> To pour in torrents."

The legend of Savage Island places Maui in the role of fire-maker. He has stolen fire in the underworld. His father tries to catch him, but Maui sets fire to the bushes by the path until a great conflagration is raging which pursues him to the upper-world.

Some legends make Maui the fire-teacher as well as the fire-finder. He teaches men how to use hardwood sticks in the fine dry dust on the bark of certain trees, or how to use the fine fibre of the palm tree to catch sparks.

In Tahiti the fire god lived in the "Hale-a-o-a," or House of the Banyan. Sometimes human sacrifices were placed upon the sacred branches of this tree of the fire god.

In the Bowditch or Fakaofa Islands the goddess of fire when conquered taught not only the method of making fire by friction but also what fish were to be cooked and what were to be eaten raw.

Thus some of the myths of Maui, the mischievous, finding fire are told by the side of the inrolling surf, while natives of many islands, around their poi bowls, rest in the shade of the far-reaching boughs and thick foliage of the banyan and other fire producing trees.

VI

Maui the Skillful

According to the New Zealand legends there were six Mauis-the Hawaiians counted four. They were a band of brothers. The older five were known as "the forgetful Mauis." The tricky and quick-witted youngest member of the family was called Maui te atamai—"Maui the skillful."

He was curiously accounted for in the New Zealand under-world. When he went down through the long cave to his ancestor's home to find fire, he was soon talked about. "Perhaps this is the man about whom so much is said in the upper-world." His ancestress from whom be obtained fire recognized him as the man called "the deceitful Maui." Even his parents told him once, "We know you are a tricky fellow-more so than any other man." One of the New Zealand fire legends while recording his flight to the under-world and his appearance as a bird, says: "The men tried to spear him, and to catch him in nets. At last they cried out, 'Maybe you are the man whose fame is great in the upper-world.' At once he leaped to the ground and appeared in the form of a man."

He was not famous for inventions, but he was always ready to improve upon anything which was already in existence. He could take the sun in hand and make it do better work. He could tie the moon so that it had to swim back around the island to the place in the ocean from which it might rise again, and go slowly through the night.

His brothers invented a slender, straight and smooth spear with which to kill birds. He saw the fluttering, struggling birds twist themselves off the smooth point and escape. He made a good light bird spear and put notches in it and kept most of the birds stuck. His brothers finally examined his spear and learned the reason for its superiority. In the same way they learned how to spear fish. They could strike and wound and sometimes kill—but they could not with their smooth spears draw the fish from the waters of the coral caves. But Maui the youngest made barbs, so that the fish could not easily shake themselves loose. The others soon made their spears like his.

The brothers were said to have invented baskets in which to trap eels, but many eels escaped. Maui improved the basket by secretly making an inside partition as well as a cover, and the eels were securely trapped. It took the brothers a long time to learn the real difference between their baskets and his. One of the family made a basket like his and caught many eels. Then Maui became angry and chanted a curse over him and bewildered him, then changed him into a dog.

The Manahiki Islanders have the legend that Maui made the moon, but could not get good light from it. He tried experiments and found that the sun was quite an improvement. The sun's example stimulated the moon to shine brighter.

Once Maui became interested in tattooing and tried to make a dog look better by placing dark lines around the mouth. The legends say that one of the sacred birds saw the pattern and then marked the sky with the red lines sometimes seen at sunrise and sunset. An Hawaiian legend says that Maui tattooed his arm with a sacred name and thus that arm was strong enough to hold the sun when he lassoed it. There is a New Zealand legend in which Maui is made one of three gods who first created man and then woman from one of the man's ribs.

The Hawaiians dwelling in Hilo have many stories of Maui. They say that his home was on the northern bank of the Wailuku River. He had a strong staff made from, an ohia tree (the native apple tree). With this he punched holes through the lava, making natural bridges and boiling pools, and new channels for its sometimes obstructed waters, so that the people could go up or down the river more easily. Near one of the natural bridges is a figure of the moon carved in the rocks, referred by some of the natives to Maui.

Maui is said to have taught his brothers the different kinds of fish nets and the use of the strong fibre of the olona, which was much better than cocoanut threads.

The New Zealand stories relate the spear-throwing contests of Maui and his brothers. As children, however, they were not allowed the use of wooden spears. They took the stems of long, heavy reeds and threw them at each other, but Maui's reeds were charmed into stronger and harder fibre so that he broke his mother's house and made her recognize him as one of her children. He had been taken away as soon as he was born by the gods to whom he was related. When he found his way back home his mother paid no attention to him. Thus by a spear thrust he won a home.

The brothers all made fish hooks, but Maui the youngest made two kinds of hooks—one like his brothers' and one with a sharp barb. His brothers' hooks were smooth so that it was difficult to keep the fish from floundering and shaking themselves off, but they noticed that the fish were held by Maui's hook better than by theirs. Maui was not inclined to devote himself to hard work, and lived on his brothers as much as possible—but when driven out by his wife or his mother he would catch more fish than the other fishermen. They tried to examine his hooks, but he always changed his hooks so that they could not see any difference between his and theirs. At such times they called him the mischievous one and tried to leave him behind while they went fishing. They were, however, always ready to give him credit for his improvements. They dealt generously with him when they learned what he had really accom, plished. When they caught him with his barbed hook they forgot the past and called him "ke atamai"—the skillful.

The idea that fish hooks made from the jawbones of human beings were better than others, seemed to have arisen at first from the angle formed in the lower jawbone. Later these human fish hooks were considered sacred and therefore possessed of magic powers. The greater sanctity and power belonged to the bones which bore more especial relation to the owner. Therefore Maui's "magic hook," with which he fished up islands, was made from the jawbone of his ancestress Malmika. It is also said that in order to have powerful hooks for every-day fishing he killed two of his children. Their right eyes he threw tip into the sky to become stars. One became the morning and the other the evening star.

The idea that the death of any members of the family must not stand in the way of obtaining magical power, has prevailed throughout Polynesia. From this angle in the jawbone Maui must have conceived the idea of making a hook with a piece of bone or shell which should be fastened to the large bone at a very sharp angle, thus making a kind of barb. Hooks like this have been made for ages among the Polynesians.

Maui and his brothers went fishing for eels with bait strung on the flexible rib of a cocoanut leaf. The stupid brothers did not fasten the ends of the string. Therefore the eels easily slipped the bait off and escaped. But Maui made the ends of his string fast, and captured many eels.

The little things which others did not think about were the foundation of Maui's fame. Upon these little things he built his courage to snare the sun and seek fire for mankind.

In a New Zealand legend, quoted by Edward Tregear, Maui is called Maui-maka-walu, or "Maui with eyes eight." This eight-eyed Maui would be allied to the Hindoo deities who with their eight eyes face the four quarters of the world-thus possessing both insight into the affairs of men and foresight into the future.

Fornander, the Hawaiian ethnologist, says: "In Hawaiian mythology, Kamapuaa, the demi-god opponent of the goddess Pele, is described as having eight eyes and eight feet; and in the legends Maka-walu, 'eight-eyed,' is a frequent epithet of gods and chiefs." He notes this coincidence with the appearance of some of the principal Hindoo deities as having some bearing upon the origin of the Polynesians. It may be that a comparative study of the legends of other islands of the Pacific by some student will open up other new and important facts.

In Tahiti, on the island Raiatea, a high priest or prophet lived in the long, long ago. He was known as Maui the prophet of Tahiti. He was probably not Maui the demi-god. Nevertheless he was represented as possessing very strange prophetical powers.

According to the historian Ellis, who previous to 1830 spent eight years in the Society and Hawaiian Islands, this prophet Maui clearly prophesied the coming of an outriggerless canoe from some foreign land. An outrigger is a log which so balances a canoe that it can ride safely through the treacherous surf.

The chiefs and prophets charged him with stating the impossible.

He took his wooden calabash and placed it in a pool of water as an illustration of the way such a boat should float.

Then with the floating bowl before him he uttered the second prophecy, that boats without line to tie the sails to the masts, or the masts to the ships, should also come to Tahiti.

When English ships under Captain Wallis and Captain Cook, in the latter part of the eighteenth century, visited these islands, the natives cried out, "O the canoes of Maui—the outriggerless canoes."

Passenger steamships, and the men-of-war from the great nations, have taught the Tahitians that boats without sails and masts can cross the great ocean, and again they have recurred to the words of the prophet Maui, and have exclaimed, "O the boats without sails and masts." This rather remarkable prophecy could easily have occurred to Maui as he saw a wooden calabash floating over rough waters.

Maui's improvement upon nature's plan in regard to certain birds is also given in the legends as a proof of his supernatural powers.

White relates the story as follows: "Maui requested some birds to go and fetch water for him. The first one would not obey, so he threw it into the water. He requested another bird to go-and it refused, so he threw it into the fire, and its feathers were burnt. But the next bird obeyed, but could not carry the water, and he rewarded it by making the feathers of the fore part of its head white. Then he asked another bird to go, and it filled its ears with water and brought it to Maui, who drank, and then pulled the bird's legs and made them long in payment for its act of kindness."

Diffenbach says: "Maui, the Adam of New Zealand, left the cat's cradle to the New Zealanders as an inheritance." The name "Whai" was given to the game. It exhibited the various steps of creation according to Maori mythology. Every change in the cradle shows some act in creation. Its various stages were called "houses." Diffenbach says again: "In this game of Maui they are great proficients. It is a game like that called cat's cradle in Europe. It is intimately connected with their ancient traditions and in the different figures which the cord is made to assume whilst held on both hands, the outline of their different varieties of houses, canoes or figures of men and women are imagined to be represented." One writer connects this game with witchcraft, and says it was brought from the under-world. Some parts of the puzzle show the adventures of Maui, especially his attempt to win immortality for men.

In New Zealand it was said Maui found a large, fine-grained stone block, broke it in pieces, and from the fragments learned how to fashion stone implements.

White also tells the New Zealand legend of Maui and the winds.

"Maui caught and held all the winds save the west wind. He put each wind into a cave, so that it might not blow. He sought in vain for the west wind, but could not find from whence it came. If he had found the cave in which it stayed he would have closed the entrance to that cave with rocks. When the west wind blows lightly it is because Maui has got near to it, and has nearly caught it, and it has gone into its home, the cave, to escape him. When the winds of the south, east, and north blow furiously it is because the rocks have been removed by the stupid people who could not learn the lessons taught by Maui. At other times Maui allows these winds to blow in hurricanes to punish that people, and also that he may ride on these furious winds in search of the west wind."

In the Hawaiian legends Maui is represented as greatly interested in making and flying kites. His favorite place for the sport was by the boiling pools of the Wailuku river near Hilo. He had the winds under his control and would call for them to push his kites in the direction he wished. His incantation calling up the winds is given in this Maui proverb-

"Strong wind come,
Soft wind come."

White in his "Ancient History of the Maoris," relates some of Maui's experiences with the people whom he found on the islands brought up from the under-world. On one island he found a sand house with eight hundred gods living in it. Apparently Maui discovered islands with inhabitants, and was reported to have fished them up out of the depths of the ocean. Fishing was sailing over the ocean until distant lands were drawn near or "fished up."

Maui walked over the islands and found men living on them and fires burning near their homes. He evidently did not know much about fire, for he took it in his hands. He was badly burned and rushed into the sea. Down he dived under the cooling waters and came up with one of the New Zealand islands on his shoulders. But his hands were still burning, so wherever he held the island it was set on fire.

These fires are still burning in the secret recesses of the volcanoes, and sometimes burst out in flowing lava. Then Maui paid attention to the people whom he had fished up. He tried to teach them, but they did not learn as he thought they should. He quickly became angry and said, "It is a waste of light for the sun to shine on such stupid people." So he tried to hold his hands between them and the sun, but the rays of the sun were too many and too strong; there fore, he could not shut them out. Then he tried the moon and managed to make it dark a part of the time each month. In this way he made a little trouble for the stupid people.

There are other hints in the legends concerning Maui's desire to be revenged upon any one who incurred his displeasure. It was said that Maui for a time lived in the heavens above the earth. Here he had a foster brother Maru. The two were cultivating the fields. Maru sent a snowstorm over Maui's field. (It would seem as if this might be a Polynesian memory of a cold land where their ancestors knew the cold winter, or a lesson learned from the snow-caps of high mountains.) At any rate, the snow blighted Maui's crops. Maui retaliated by praying for rain to destroy Maru's fields. But Maru managed to save a part of his crops. Other legends make Maui the aggressor. At the last, however, Maui became very angry. The foster parents tried to soothe the two men by saying, "Live in peace with each other and do not destroy each other's food." But Maui was implacable and lay in wait for his foster brother, who was in the habit of carrying fruit and grass as an offering to the gods of a temple situated on the summit of a hill. Here Maui killed Maru and then went away to the earth.

This legend is told by three or four different, tribes of New Zealand and is very similar to the Hebrew story of Cain and Abel. At this late day it is difficult to say definitely whether or not it owes its origin to the early touch of Christianity upon New Zealand when white men first began to live with the natives. It is somewhat similar to stories found in the Tonga Islands and also in the Hawaiian group, where a son of the first gods, or rather of the first men, kills a brother. In each case there is the shadow of the Biblical idea. It seems safe to infer that such legends are not entirely drawn from contact with Christian civilization. The natives claim that these stories are very ancient, and that their fathers knew them before the white men sailed on the Pacific.

VII

Maui and Tuna

When Maui returned from the voyages in which he discovered or "fished up" from the ocean depths new islands, he gave deep thought to the things he had found. As the islands appeared to come out of the water he saw they were inhabited. There were houses and stages for drying and preserving food. He was greeted by barking dogs. Fires were burning, food cooking and people working. He evidently had gone so far away from home that a strange people was found. The legend which speaks of the death of his brothers, "eaten" by the great fish drawn up from the floor of the sea, may very easily mean that the new people killed and ate the brothers.

Maui apparently learned some new lessons, for on his return he quickly established a home of his own, and determined to live after the fashion of the families in the new islands.

Maui sought Hina-a-te-lepo, "daughter of the swamp," and secured her as his wife. The New Zealand tribes tell legends which vary in different localities about this woman Hina. She sometimes bore the name Rau-kura—"The red plume."

She cared for his thatched house as any other Polynesian woman was in the habit of doing. She attempted the hurried task of cooking his food before he snared the sun and gave her sufficient daylight for her labors.

They lived near the bank of a river from which Hina was in the habit of bringing water for the household needs.

One day she went down to the stream with her calabash. She was entwined with wreaths of leaves and flowers, as was the custom among Polynesian women. While she was standing on the bank, Tuna-roa, "the long eel," saw her. He swam up to the bank and suddenly struck her and knocked her into the water and covered her with slime from the blow given by his tail.

Hina escaped and returned to her home, saying nothing to Maui about the trouble. But the next day, while getting water, she was again overthrown and befouled by the slime of Tuna-roa.

Then Hina became angry and reported the trouble to Maui.

Maui decided to punish the long eel and started out to find his hiding place. Somie of the New Zealand legends as collected by White, state that Tuna-roa was a very smooth skinned chief, who lived on the opposite bank of the stream, and, seeing Hina, had insulted her.

When Maui saw this chief, he caught two pieces of wood over which he was accustomed to slide his canoe into the sea. These he carried to the stream and laid them from bank to bank as a bridge over which he might entice Tuna-roa to cross.

Maui took his stone axe, Ma-Tori-Tori, "the severer," and concealed himself near the bank of the river.

When "the long eel" had crossed the stream, Maui rushed out and killed him with a mighty blow of the stone axe, cutting the head from the body.

Other legends say that Maui found Tuna-roa living as an eel in a deep water hole, in a swamp on the seacoast of Tata-a, part of the island Ao-tea-roa. Other stories located Tuna-roa in the river near Maui's home.

Maui saw that he could not get at his enemy without letting off the water which protected him.

Therefore into the forest went Maui, and with sacred ceremonies, selected trees from the wood of which he prepared tools and weapons.

Meanwhile, in addition to the insult given to Hina, Tuna-roa had caught and devoured two of Maui's children, which made Maui more determined to kill him.

Maui made the narrow spade (named by the Maoris of New Zealand the "ko," and by the Hawaiians "o-o") and the sharp spears, with which to pierce either the earth or his enemy. These spears and spades were consecrated to the work of preparing a ditch by which to draw off the water protecting "the long eel."

The work of trench-making was accomplished with many incantations and prayers. The ditch was named "The sacred digging," and was tabooed to all other purposes except that of catching Tuna-roa.

Across this ditch Maui stretched a strong net, and then began a new series of chants and ceremonies to bring down an abundance of rain. Soon the flood came and the overflowing waters rushed down the sacred ditch. The walls of the deep pool gave way and "the long eel" was carried down the trench into the waiting net. Then there was commotion. Tuna-roa was struggling for freedom.

Maui saw him and hastened to grasp his stone axe, "the severer." Hurrying to the net, he struck Tuna-roa a terrible blow, and cut off the head. With a few more blows, he cut the body in pieces. The head and tail were carried out into the sea. The head became fish and the tail became the great conger-eel. Other parts of the body became sea monsters. But some parts which fell in fresh water became the common eels. From the hairs of the head came certain vines and creepers among the plants.

After the death of Tuna-roa the offspring of Maui were in no danger of being killed and soon multiplied into a large family.

Another New Zealand legend related by White says that Maui built a sliding place of logs, over which Tuna-roa must pass when coming from the river.

Maui also made a screen behind which he could secrete himself while watching for Tuna-roa.

He commanded Hina to come down to the river and wait on the bank to attract Tuna-roa. Soon the long eel was seen in the water swimming near to Hina. Hina went to a place back of the logs which Maui had laid down.

Tuna-roa came towards her, and began to slide down the skids.

Maui sprang out from his hiding place and killed Tuna-roa with his axe, and cut him in pieces.

The tail became the conger-eel. Parts of his body became fresh-water eels. Some of the blood fell upon birds and always after marked them with red spots. Some of the blood was thrown into certain trees, making this wood always red. The muscles became vines and creepers.

From this time the children of Maui caught and ate the eels of both salt and fresh water. Eel traps were made, and Maui taught the people the proper chants or incantations to use when catching eels.

This legend of Maui and the long eel was found by White in a number of forms among the different tribes of New Zealand, but does not seem to have had currency in many other island groups.

In Turner's "Samoa" a legend is related which was probably derived from the Maui stories and yet differs in its romantic results. The Samoans say that among their ancient ones dwelt a woman named Sina. Sina among the Polynesians is the same as Hina—the "h" is softened into "s". She captured a small eel and kept it as a pet. It grew large and strong and finally attacked and bit her. She fled, but the eel followed her everywhere. Her father came to her assistance and raised high mountains between the eel and herself.

But the eel passed over the barrier and pursued her. Her mother raised a new series of mountains. But again the eel surmounted the difficulties and attempted to seize Sina. She broke away from him and ran on and on. Finally she wearily passed through a village. The people asked her to stay and eat with them, but she said they could only help her by delivering her from the pursuing eel. The inhabitants of that village were afraid of the eel and refused to fight for her. So she ran on to another place. Here the chief offered her a drink of water and promised to kill the eel for her. He prepared awa, a stupefying drink, and put poison in it. When the eel came along the chief asked him to drink. He took the awa and prepared to follow Sina. When he came to the place where she was the pains of death had already seized him. While dying he begged her to bury his head by her home. This she did, and in time a plant new to the islands sprang up. It became a tree, and finally produced a cocoanut, whose two eyes could continually look into the face of Sina.

Tuna, in the legends of Fiji, was a demon of the sea. He lived in a deep sea cave, into which he sometimes shut himself behind closed doors of coral. When he was hungry, he swam through the ocean shadows, always watching the restless surface. When a canoe passed above him, he would throw himself swiftly through the waters, upset the canoe, and seize some of the boatmen and devour them. He was greatly feared by all the fishermen of the Fijian coasts.

Roko—a mo-o or dragon god—in his journey among the islands, stopped at a village by the sea and asked for a canoe and boatmen. The people said: "We have nothing but a very old canoe out there by the water." He went to it and found it in a very bad condition. He put it in the water, and decided that he could use it. Then he asked two men to go with him and paddle, but they refused because of fear, and explained this fear by telling the story of the water demon, who continually sought the destruction of this canoe, and also their own death. Roko encouraged them to take him to wage battle with Tuna, telling them he would destroy the monster. They paddled until they were directly over Tuna's cave. Roko told them to go off to one side and wait and watch, saying: "I am going down to see this Tuna. If you see red blood boil up through the water, you may be sure that Tuna has been killed. If the blood is black, then you will know that he has the victory and I am dead."

Roko leaped into the water and went down—down to the door of the cave. The coral doors were closed. He grasped them in his strong hands and tore them open, breaking them in pieces. Inside he found cave after cave of coral, and broke his way through until at last he awoke

Tuna. The angry demon cried: "Who is that?" Roko answered: "It is I, Roko, alone. Who are you?"

Tuna aroused himself and demanded Roko's business and who guided him to that place. Roko replied: "No one has guided me. I go from place to place, thinking that there is no one else in the world."

Tuna shook himself angrily. "Do you think I am nothing? This day is your last."

Roko replied: "Perhaps so. If the sky falls, I shall die."

Tuna leaped upon Roko and bit him. Then came the mighty battle of the coral caves. Roko broke Tuna into several pieces—and the red blood poured in boiling bubbles upward through the clear ocean waters, and the boatmen cried: "The blood is red the blood is red—Tuna is dead by the hand of Roko."

Roko lived for a time in Fiji, where his descendants still find their home. The people use this chant to aid them in difficulties:

"My load is a red one.
It points in front to Kawa (Roko's home).
Behind, it points to Dolomo—(a village on another island)."

In the Hawaiian legends, Hina was Maui's mother rather than his wife, and Kuna (Tuna) was a mo-o, a dragon or gigantic lizard possessing miraculous powers.

Hina's home was in the large cave under the beautiful Rainbow Falls near the city of Hilo. Above the falls the bed of the river is along the channel of an ancient lava flow. Sometimes the water pours in a torrent over the rugged lava, sometimes it passes through underground passages as well as along the black river bed, and sometimes it thrusts itself into boiling pools.

Maui lived on the northern side of the river, but a chief named Kuna-moo—a dragon—lived in the boiling pools. He attacked Hina and threw a dam across the river below Rainbow Falls, intending to drown Hina in her cave. The great ledge of rock filled the river bed high up the bank on the Hilo side of the river. Hina called on Maui for aid. Maui came quickly and with mighty blows cut out a new channel for the river—the path it follows to this day. The waters sank and Hina remained unharmed in her cave.

The place where Kuna dwelt was called Wai-kuna—the Kuna water. The river in which Hina and Kuna dwelt bears the name Wailuku—"the destructive water." Maui went above Kuna's home and poured hot water into the river. This part of the myth could easily have arisen from a lava outburst on the side of the volcano above the river. The hot water swept in a flood over Kuna's home. Kuna jumped from the boiling pools over a series of small falls near his home into the river below. Here the hot water again scalded him and in pain he leaped from the river to the bank, where Maui killed him by beating him with a club. His body was washed down the river over the falls under which Hina dwelt, into the ocean.

The story of Kuna or Tuna is a legend with a foundation in the enmity between two chiefs of the long ago, and also in a desire to explain the origin of the family of eels and the invention of nets and traps.

VIII

Maui and His Brother-in-Law

The "Stories of Maui's Brother-in-Law," and of "Maui seeking Immortality," are not found in Hawaiian mythology. We depend upon Sir George Grey and John White for the New Zealand myths in which both of these legends occur.

Maui's sister Hina-uri married Ira-waru, who was willing to work with his skillful brother-in-law. They hunted in the forests and speared birds. They fished and farmed together. They passed through many experiences similar to those Maui's own brothers had suffered before the brother-in-law took their place as Maui's companion. They made spears together—but Maui made notched barbs for his spear ends—and slipped them off when Ira-waru came near. So for a long time the proceeds of bird hunting fell to Maui. But after a time the brother-in-law learned the secret as the brothers had before, and Maui was looked up to by his fellow hunter as the skillful one. Sometimes Ira-waru was able to see at once Maui's plan and adopt it. He discovered Maui's method of making the punga or eel baskets for catching eels.

The two hunters went to the forest to find a certain creeping vine with which to weave their eel snares. Ira-waru made a basket with a hole, by which the eels could enter, but they could turn around and go out the same way. So he very seldom caught an eel. But Maui made his basket with a long funnelshaped door, by which the eels could easily slide into the snare but could scarcely escape. He made a door in the side which he fastened tight until he wished to pour the eels out.

Ira-waru immediately made a basket like Maui. Then Maui became angry and uttered incantations over Ira-waru. The man dropped on the ground and became a dog. Maui returned home and met his sister, who charged him with sorcery concerning her husband.

Maui did not deny the exercise of his power, but taught his sister a chant and sent her out to the level country. There she uttered her chant and a strange dog with long hair came to her, barking and leaping around her. Then she knew what Maui had done. "Thus Ira-waru became the first of the long-haired dogs whose flesh has been tabooed to women."

The Tahu and Han tribes of New Zealand tell a different story. They say that Maui went to visit Ira-waru. Together they set out on a journey. After a time they rested by the wayside and became sleepy. Maui asked Ira-waru to cleanse his head. This gave him the restful, soothing touch which aided sleep. Then Maui proposed that Ira-waru sleep. Taking the head in his hands, Maui put his brother-in-law to sleep. Then by incantations he made the sleep very deep and prolonged. Meanwhile he pulled the ears and arms and limbs until they were properly lengthened. He drew out the under jaw until it had the form of a dog's mouth. He stretched the end of the backbone into a tail, and then wakened Ira-waru and drove him back when he tried to follow the path to the settlement.

Hina-uri went out and called her husband. He came to her, leaping and barking. She decided that this was her husband, and in her agony reproached Maui and wandered away.

The Rua-nui story-tellers of New Zealand say that Maui's anger was aroused against Ira-waru because he ate all the bait when they went fishing, and they could catch no fish after paddling out to the fishing grounds. When they carne to land, Maui told Irawarn to lie down in the sand as a roller over which to drag the canoe up the beach. When he was lying helpless under the canoe, Maui changed him into a dog.

The Arawa legends make the cause of Maui's anger the success of Ira-waru while fishing. Ira-waru had many fish while Maui had captured but few. The story is told thus: "Ira-waru hooked a fish and in pulling it in his line became entangled with that of Maui. Maui felt the jerking and began to pull in his line. Soon they pulled their lines close up to the canoe, one to the bow, the other to the stern, where each was sitting. Maui said: 'Let me pull the lines to me, as the fish is on my hook.' His brother-in-law said: 'Not so; the fish is on mine.' But Maui said: 'Let me pull my line in.' Ira-waru did so and saw that the fish was on his hook. Then he said: 'Untwist your lines and let mine go, that I may pull the fish in.' Maui said: I will do so, but let me have time.' He took the fish off Ira-waru's hook and saw that there was a barb on the hook. He said to Ira-waru: 'Perhaps we ought to return to land! When they were dragging the canoe on shore, Maui said to Ira-waru: 'Get between the canoe and outrigger and drag.' Irawaru did so and Maui leaped on the outrigger and weighed it heavily down and crushed Ira-waru prostrate on the beach. Maui trod on him and pulled his backbone long like a tail and changed him into a dog."

Maui is said to have tattooed the muzzle of the dog with a beautiful pattern which the birds (kahui-zara, a flock of tern) used in marking the sky. From this also came the red glow which sometimes flushes the face of man.

Another Arawa version of the legend was that Mau and Ira-waru were journeying together. Ira-waru wa gluttonous and ate the best food. At last Maui determined to punish his companion. By incantation lengthened the way until Ira-waru became faint an weary. Maui had provided himself with a little food and therefore was enabled to endure the long way. While Ira-waru slept Maui trod on his backbone and lengthened it and changed the arms and limbs into the legs of a dog. When Hina-uri saw the state of her husband she went into the thatched house by which Ira-waru had so often stood watching the hollow log in which she dried the fish and preserved the birds speared in the mountains. She bound her girdle and hala-leaf apron around her and went down to the sea to drown herself, that her body might be eaten by the monsters of the sea. When she came to the shell-covered beach, she sat down and sang her death song—

"I weep, I call to the steep billows of the sea
And to him, the great, the ocean god;
To monsters, all now hidden,
To come and bury me,
Who now am wrapped in mourning.
Let the waves wear their mourning, too,
And sleep as sleeps the dead."

—Ancient Maui Chant of New Zealand

Then Hina-uri threw herself into the sea and was borne on the waves many moons, at last drifting to shore, to be found by two fishermen. They carried the body off to the fire and warmed it back to life. They brushed off the sea moss and sea weeds and rubbed her until she awoke.

Soon they told their chief, Tini-rau, what a beautiful woman they had found in the sea. He came and took her away to make her one of his wives. But the other wives were jealous and drove Hina-uri away from the chief's houses.

Another New Zealand legend says that Hina came to the sea and called for a little fish to aid her in going away from the island. It tried to carry her, but was too weak. Hina struck it with her open hand. It had striped sides forever after. She tried a larger fish, but fell off before they had gone far from shore. Her blow gave this fish its beautiful blue spots. Another received black spots. Another she stamped her foot upon, making it flat. At last a shark carried her far away. She was very thirsty, and broke a cocoanut on the shark's head, making a bump, which has been handed down for generations. The shark carried her to the home of the two who rescued her and gave her new strength.

Meanwhile Rupe or Maui-mua, a brother of Hinauri and Maui, grieved for his sister. He sought for her throughout the land and then launched his canoe upon the blue waters surrounding Ao-tea-roa (The Great White Land; the ancient native New Zealand) and searched the coasts. He only learned that his sister had, as the natives said, "leaped into the waters and been carried away into the heavens."

Rupe's heart filled with the desire to find and protect the frenzied sister who had probably taken a canoe and floated away, out of the horizon, seen from New Zealand coasts, into new horizons. During the Viking age of the Pacific, when many chiefs sailed long distances, visiting the most remote islands of Polynesia, they frequently spoke of breaking through from the home land into new heavens-or of climbing up the path of the sun on the waters into a new heaven. This was their poetical way of passing from horizon to horizon. The horizon around their particular island surrounded their complete world. Outside, somewhere, were other worlds and other heavens. Rupe's voyage was an idyll of the Pacific. It was one more story to be added to the prose poems of consecrated travel. It was a brother feeling through the mysteries of unknown lands for a sister, as dear to him as an Evangeline has been to other men.

From the mist-land of the Polynesian race comes this story of the trickery of Maui the learned, and the faithfulness of his older brother Maui-mua or Rupe-one of the "five forgetful Mauis." Rupe hoisted mat-sails over his canoe and thus made the winds serve him. He paddled the canoe onward through the hotlis when calms rested on glassy waves.

Thus he passed out of sight of Ao-tea-roa, away from his brothers, and out of the reach of all tricks and incantations of Maui, the mischievous. He sailed until a new island rose out of the sea to greet him. Here in a "new heaven" he found friends to care for him and prepare him for his longer journey. His restless anxiety for his sister urged him onward until days lengthened into months and months into years. He passed from the horizons of newly-discovered islands, into the horizons of circling skies around islands of which he had never heard before. Sometimes he found relatives, but more frequently his welcome came from those who could trace no historical touch in their genealogies.

Here and there, apparently, he found traces of a woman whose description answered that of his sister Hina-uri. At last he looked through the heavens upon a new world, and saw his sister in great trouble.

According to some legends the jealous wives of the great chief, Tini-rau, attack Hina, who was known among them as Hina-te-ngaru-moana, "Hina, the daughter of the ocean." Tini-rau and Hina lived away from the village of the chief until their little boy was born. When they needed food, the chief said, "Let us go to my settlement and we shall have food provided."

But Hina chanted:

"Let it down, let it down,
Descend, oh! descend—"

and sufficient food fell before them. After a time their frail clothing wore out, and the cold chilled them, then Hina again uttered the incantation and clothing was provided for their need.

But the jealous wives, two in number, finally heard where Hina and the chief were living, and started to see them.

Tini-rau said to Hina, "Here come my other wives—be careful how you act before them."

She replied, "If they come in anger it will be evil."

She armed herself with an obsidian or volcanic-glass knife, and waited their coming.

They tried to throw enchantments around her to, kill her. Then one of them made a blow at her with a weapon, but she turned it aside and killed her enemy with the obsidian knife.

Then the other wife made an attack, and again the obsidian knife brought death. She ripped open the stomachs of the jealous ones and showed the chief fish lines and sinkers and other property which they had eaten in the past and which Tini-rau had never been able to trace.

Another legend says that the two women came to kill Hina when they heard of the birth of her boy. For a time she was greatly terrified. Then she saw that they were coming from different directions. She attacked the nearest one with a stone and killed her. The body burst open, and was seen to be full of green stone. Then she killed the second wife in the same way, and found more green stones. "Thus, according to the legends, originated the greenstone" from which the choicest and most valuable stone tools have since been made. For a time the chief and Hina lived happily together. Then he began to neglect her and abuse her, until she cried aloud for her brother—

"O Rupe! come down.
Take me and my child."

Rupe assumed the form of a bird and flew down to this world in which he had found his sister. He chanted as he came down—

"It is Rupe, yes Rupe,
The elder brother;
And I am here."

He folded the mother and her boy under his wings and flew away with them. Sir George Gray relates a legend in which Maui-mua or Rupe is recorded as having carried his sister and her child to one of the new lands, found in his long voyage, where dwelt an aged relative, of chief rank, with his retainers.

Some legends say that Tini-rau tried to catch Rupe, who was compelled to drop the child in order to escape with the mother. Tini-rau caught the child and carefully cared for him until he grew to be a strong young lad.

Then he wanted to find his mother and bring her back to his father. How this was done, how Rupe took his sister back to the old chief, and how civil wars arose are not all these told in the legends of the Maoris. Thus the tricks of Maui the mischievous brought trouble for a time, but were finally overshadowed by happy homes in neighboring lands for his suffering sister and her descendants.

IX

Maui's Kite Flying

Maui the demi-god was sometimes the Hercules of Polynesia. His exploits were fully as marvelous as those of the hero of classic mythology. He snared the sun. He pulled up islands from the ocean depths. He lifted the sky into its present position and smoothed its arched surface with his stone adze. These stories belong to all Polynesia.

There are numerous less important local myths, some of them peculiar to New Zealand, some to the Society Islands and some to the Hawaiian group.

One of the old native Hawaiians says that in the long, long ago the birds were flying around the homes of the ancient people. The flutter of their wings could be heard and the leaves and branches moved when the motion of the wings ceased and the wanderers through the air found resting places. Then came sweet music from the trees and the people marvelled. Only one of all mankind could see the winged warblers. Maui, the demi-god, had clear vision. The swift-flying wings covered with red or gold he saw. The throats tinted many colors and reflecting the sunlight with diamond sparks of varied hues he watched while they trembled with the melody of sweet bird songs. All others heard but did not see. They were blind and yet had open vision.

Sometimes the iiwi (a small red bird) fluttered in the air and uttered its shrill, happy song, and Maui saw and heard. But the bird at that time was without color in the eyes of the ancient people and only the clear voice was heard, while no speck of bird life flecked the clear sky overhead.

At one time a god from one of the other islands came to visit Maui. Each boasted of and described the beauties and merits of his island. While they were conversing, Maui called for his friends the birds. They gathered around the house and fluttered among the leaves of the surrounding trees. Soon their sweet voices filled the air on all sides. All the people wondered and worshiped, thinking they heard the fairy or menchune people. It was said that Maui had painted the bodies of his invisible songsters and for a long time had kept the delight of their flashing colors to himself. But when the visitor had rejoiced in the mysterious harmonies, Maui decided to take away whatever veil shut out the sight of these things beautiful, that his bird friends might be known and honored ever after. So he made the birds reveal themselves perched in the trees or flying in the air. The clear eyes of the god first recognized the new revelation, then all the people became dumb before the sweet singers adorned in all their brilliant tropical plumage.

The beautiful red birds, iiwi and akakani, and the birds of glorious yellow feathers, the oo and the mamo, were a joy to both eye and ear and found high places in Hawaiian legend and story, and all gave their most beautiful feathers for the cloaks and helmets of the chiefs.

The Maoris of New Zealand say that Maui could at will change himself into a bird and with his feathered friends find a home in leafy shelters. In bird form he visited the gods of the under-world. His capricious soul was sensitive to the touch of all that mysterious life of nature.

With the birds as companions and the winds as his servants Maui must soon have turned his inventive mind to kite making.

The Hawaiian myths are perhaps the only ones of the Pacific Ocean which give to any of the gods the pleasure and excitement of kite flying. Maui, after repeated experiments, made a large kite for himself. It was much larger than any house of his time or generation. He twisted a long line from the strong fibers of the native plant known as the olona. He endowed both kite and string with marvelous powers and launched the kite up toward the clouds. It rose very slowly. The winds were not lifting it into the sky.

Maui remembered that an old priest lived in Waipio valley, the largest and finest valley of the large island, Hawaii, on which he made his home.

This priest had a covered calabash in which he compelled the winds to hide when he did not wish them to play on land and sea. The priest's name was Kaleiioku, and his calabash was known as ipu-makania ka maumau, "the calabash of the perpetual winds." Maui called for the priest who had charge of the winds to open his calabash and let them come up to Hilo and blow along the Wailuku river. The natives say that the place where Maui stood was marked by the pressure of his feet in the lava rocks of the river bank as he braced himself to hold the kite against the increasing force of the winds which pushed it towards the sky. Then the enthusiasm of kite flying filled his youthful soul and he cried aloud, screaming his challenge along the coast of the sea toward Waipio—

"O winds, winds of Waipio,
In the calabash of Kaleiioku.
Come from the ipu-makard,
O wind, the wind of Hilo,
Come quickly, come with power."

Then the priest lifted the cover of the calabash of the winds and let the strong winds of Hilo escape. Along the sea coast they rushed until as they entered Hilo Bay they heard the voice of Maui calling—

"O winds, winds of Hilo,
Hasten and come to me."

With a tumultuous rush the strong winds turned toward the mountains. They forced their way along the gorges and palisades of the Wailuku river. They leaped into the heavens, making a fierce attack upon the monster which Maui had sent into the sky. The kite struggled as it was pushed upward by the hands of the fierce winds, but Maui rejoiced. His heart was uplifted by the joy of the conflict in which his strength to hold was pitted against the power of the winds to tear away. And again he shouted toward the sea—

"O winds, the winds of Hilo,
Come to the mountains, come."

The winds which had been stirring up storms on the face of the waters came inland. They dashed against Maui. They climbed the heights of the skies until they fell with full violence against their mighty foe hanging in the heavens.

The kite had been made of the strongest kapa (paper cloth) which Maui's mother could prepare. It was not torn, although it was bent backward to its utmost limit. Then the strain came on the strong cord of olona fibre. The line was stretched and strained as the kite was pushed back. Then Maui called again and again for stronger winds to come. The cord was drawn out until the kite was far above the mountains. At last it broke and the kite was tossed over the craters of the volcanoes to the land of the district of Ka-u on the other side of the island.

Then Maui was angry and hastily leaped over the mountains, which are nearly fourteen thousand feet in altitude. In a half dozen strides he had crossed the fifty or sixty miles from his home to the place where the kite lay. He could pass over many miles with a single step. His name was Maui-Mama, "Maui the Swift." When Maui returned with his kite he was more careful in calling the winds to aid him in his sport.

The people watched their wise neighbor and soon learned that the kite could be a great blessing to them. When it was soaring in the sky there was always dry and pleasant weather. It was a day for great rejoicing. They could spread out their kapa cloth to dry as long as the kite was in the sky. They could carry out their necessary work without fear of the rain. Therefore when any one saw the kite beginning to float along the mountain side he would call out joyfully, "E! Maui's kite is in the heavens." Maui would send his kite into the blue sky and then tie the line to the great black stones in the bed of the Wailuku river.

Maui soon learned the power of his kite when blown upon by a fierce wind. With his accustomed skill he planned to make use of his strong servant, and therefore took the kite with him on his journeys to the other islands, using it to aid in making swift voyages. With the wind in the right direction, the kite could pull his double canoe very easily and quickly to its destination.

Time passed, and even the demi-god died. The fish hook with which he drew the Hawaiian Islands up from the depths of the sea was allowed to lie on the lava by the Wailuku river until it became a part of the stone. The double canoe was carried far inland and then permitted to petrify by the river side. The two stones which represent the double canoe now bear the name "Waa-Kauhi," and the kite has fallen from the sky far up on the mountain side, where it still rests, a flat plot of rich land between Mauna Kea and Mauna Loa.

X

The Oahu Legends of Maui

S everal Maui legends have been located on the island of Oahu. They were given by Mr. Kaaia to Mr. T. G. Thrum, the publisher of what is well known in the Hawaiian Islands as "Thrum's Annual." He has kindly furnished them for added interest to the present volume. The legends have a distinctly local flavor confined entirely to Oahu. It has seemed best to reserve them for a chapter by themselves although they are chiefly variations of stories already told.

Maui and the Two Gods

THIS HISTORY OF MAUI AND his grandmother Hina begins with their arrival from foreign lands. They dwelt in Kane-ana (Kane's cave), Waianae, Oahu. This is an "ana," or cave, at Puu-o-hulu. Hina had wonderful skill in making all kinds of tapa according to the custom of the women of ancient Hawaii.

Maui went to the Koolau side and rested at Kaha-luu, a diving place in Koolaupoko. In that place there is a noted hill called Ma-eli-eli. This is the story of that hill. Maui threw up a pile of dirt and concealed rubbish under it. The two gods, Kane and Kanaloa, came along and asked Maui what he was doing. He said, "What you see. You two dig on that side to the foot of the pali, (precipice) and I will go down at Kaha-luu. If you two dig through first, you may kill me. If I get through first I will kill you," They agreed, and began to dig and throw up the dirt. Then Maui dug three times and tossed up some of the hills of that place. Kane and Kanaloa saw that Maui was digging very fast, so they put forth very great strength and threw the dirt into a hill. Meanwhile Maui ran away to the other side of the island. Thus by the aid of the gods the hill Ala-eli-eli was thrown up and received its name "eli," meaning "dig." "Ma-eli-eli" meant "the place of digging."

How They Found Fire

It was said that Maui and Hina had no fire. They where often cold and had no cooked food. Maui saw flames rising in a distant place and ran to see how they were made. When he came to that place the fire was out and some birds flew away. One of them was Ka-Alae-huapi, "the stingy Alae"—a small duck, the Hawaiian mud hen. Maui watched again and saw fire. When he went up the birds saw him coming and scattered the fire, carrying the ashes into the water; but he leaped and caught the little Alae. "Ali!" he said, "I will kill you, because you do not let me have fire." The bird replied, "If you kill me you cannot find fire." Maui said, "Where is fire?" The Alae said, "Go up on the high land where beautiful plants with large leaves are standing; rub their branches." Maui set the bird free and went inland from Halawa and found dry land taro. He began to rub the stalks, but only juice came out like water. He had no red fire. He was very angry and said, "If that lying Alae is caught again by me I will be its death."

After a while he saw the fire burning and ran swiftly. The birds saw him and cried, "The cooking is over. Here comes the swift grandchild of Hina." They scattered the fire; threw the ashes away and flew into the water. But again Maui caught the Alae and began to kill it, saying: "You gave me a plant full of water from which to get fire." The bird said, "If I die you can never find fire. I will give you the secret of fire. Take a branch of that dry tree and rub." Maui held the bird fast in one hand while he rubbed with the other until smoke and fire came out. Then he took the fire stick and rubbed the head of the bird, making a place where red and white feathers have grown ever since.

He returned to Hina and taught her how to make fire, using the two fire sticks and how to twist coconut fibre to catch the fire when it had been kindled in wood. But the Alae was not forgotten. It was called huapi, "stingy," because it selfishly kept the knowledge of fire making to itself.

Maui Catching the Sun

Maui watched Hina making tapa. The wet tapa was spread on a long tapa board, and Hina began at one end to pound it into shape; pounding from one end to another. He noticed that sunset came by the time she had pounded to the middle of the board. The sun hurried so fast that she could only begin her work before the day was past.

He went to the hill Hele-a-ka-la, which means "journey of the sun." He thought he would catch the sun and make it miove slowly. He went up the hill and waited. When the sun began to rise, Maui made himself long, stretching up toward the sky. Soon the shining legs of the sun came up the hillside. He saw Maui and began to run swiftly, but Maui reached out and caught one of the legs, saying: "O sun, I will kill you. You are a mischief maker. You make trouble for Hina by going so fast." Then he broke the shining leg of the sun. The sufferer said, "I will change my way and go slowly—six months slow and six months faster." Thus arose the saying, "Long shall be the daily journey of the sun and he shall give light for all the people's toil." Hina learned that she could pound until she was tired while the farmers could plant and take care of their fields. Thus also this hill received its name Hele-a-ka-la. This is one of the hills of Waianae near the precipice of the hill Puu-o-hulu.

Uniting the Islands

MAUI SUGGESTED TO HINA THAT he had better try to draw the islands together, uniting them in one land. Hina told Maui to go and see Alae-nui-a-Hina, who would tell him what to do. The Alae told him they must go to Ponaha-ke-one (a fishing place outside of Pearl Harbor) and find Ka-uniho-kahi, "the one toothed," who held the land under the sea.

Maui went back to Hina. She told him to ask his brothers to go fishing with him. They consented and pushed out into the sea. Soon Maui saw a bailing dish floating by the canoe and picked it up. It was named Hina-a-ke-ka, "Hina who fell off." They paddled to Ponaha-ke-one. When they stopped they saw, a beautiful young wornan in the boat. Then they anchored and again looked in the boat, but the young woman was gone. They saw the bailing dish and, threw it into the sea.

Maui-mua threw his hook and caught a large fish, which was seen to be a shark as they drew it to the surface. At once they cut the line. So also Mauihope and Maui-waena. At last Maui threw his hook Manai-i-ka-lani into the sea. It went down, down into the depths. Maui cried, "Hina-a-ke-ka has my hook in her hand. By her it will be made fast." Hina went down with the hook until she met Ka-uniho-kahi. She asked him to open his mouth, then threw the hook far inside and made it fast. Then she pulled the line so that Maui should know that the fish was caught. Maui fastened the line to the outrigger of the canoe and asked his brothers to paddle with all diligence, and not look back. Long, long, they paddled and were very tired. Then Maui took a paddle and dipped deep in the sea. The boat moved more swiftly through the sea. The brothers looked back and cried, "There is plenty of land behind us." The charm was broken. The hook came out of "the one toothed," and the raised islands sank back into their place. The native say, "The islands are now united to America. Perhaps Maui has been at work."

Maui and Pea-Pea the Eight-Eyed

MAUI HAD BEEN FISHING AND had caught a great fish upon which he was feasting. He looked inland and saw his wife, Kumu-lama, seized and carried away by Pea-pea-maka-walu, "Pea-pea the eight-eyed." This is a legend derived from the myths of many islands in which Lupe or Rupe (pigeon) changed himself into a bird and flew after his sister Hina who had been carried on the back of a shark to distant islands. Sometimes as a man and sometimes as a bird he prosecuted his search until Hina was found.

Maui pursued Pea-pea, but could not catch him. He carried Maui's wife over the sea to a far away island. Maui was greatly troubled but his grandmother sent him inland to find an old man who would tell him what to do. Maui went inland and looking down toward Waipahu saw this man Ku-olo-kele. He was hump-backed. Maui threw a large stone and hit the "hill on the back" knocked it off and made the back straight. The old man lifted up the stone and threw it to Waipahu, where it lies to this day. Then he and Maui talked together. He told Maui to go and catch birds and gather ti leaves and fibers of the ie-ie vine, and fill his house. These things Maui secured and brought to him. He told Maui to go home and return after three days.

Ku-olo-kele took the ti leaves and the ie-ie threads and made the body of a great bird which he covered with bird feathers. He fastened all together with the ie-ie. This was done in the first day. The second day he placed food inside and tried his bird and it flew all right. "Thus," as the Hawaiians say, "the first flying ship was made in the time of Maui." This is a modern version of Rupe changing himself into a bird.

On the third day Maui came and saw the wonderful bird body thoroughly prepared for his journey. Maui went inside. Ku-olo-kele said, "When you reach that land, look for a village. If the people are not there look to the beach. If there are many people, your wife and

Pea-pea the eight-eyed will be there. Do not go near, but fly out over the sea. The people will say, 'O, the strange bird;' but Pea-pea will say, 'This is my bird. It is tabu.' You can then come to the people."

Maui pulled the ie-ie ropes fastened to the wings and made them move. Thus he flew away into the sky. Two days was his journey before he came to that strange island, Moana-liha-i-ka-wao-kele. It was a beautiful land. He flew inland to a village, but there were no people; according to the ancient chant:

> *"The houses of Lima-loa stand,*
> *But there are no people;*
> *They are at Mana."*

The people were by the sea. Maui flew over them. He saw his wife, but he passed on flying out over the sea, skimming like a sea bird down to the water and rising gracefully up to the sky. Pea-pea called out, "This is my bird. It is tabu." Maui heard and came to the beach. He was caught and placed in a tabu box. The servants carried him, up to the village and put him in the chief's sleeping house, when Pea-pea and his people returned to their homes.

In the night Pea-pea and Maui's wife lay down to sleep. Maui watched Pea-pea, hoping that he would soon sleep. Then he would kill him. Maui waited. One eye was closed, seven eyes were opened. Then four eyes closed, leaving three. The night was almost past and dawn was near. Then Maui called to Hina with his spirit voice, "O Hina, keep it dark." Hina made the gray dawn dark in the three eyes and two closed in sleep. The last eye was weary, and it also slept. Then Maui went out of the bird body and cut off the head of Pea-pea and put it inside the bird. He broke the roof of the house until a large opening was made. He took his wife, Kumu-lama, and flew away to the island of Oahu. The winds blew hard against the flying bird. Rain fell in torrents around it, but those inside had no trouble.

"Thus Maui returned with his wife to his home in Oahu. The story is pau (finished)."

XI

MAUI SEEKING IMMORTALITY

Climb up, climb up,
To the highest surface of heaven,
To all the sides of heaven.

Climb then to thy ancestor,
The sacred bird in the sky,
To thy ancestor Rehua

In the heavens.

—New Zealand kite incantation

The story of Maui seeking immortality for the human race is one of the finest myths in the world. For pure imagination and pathos it is difficult to find any tale from Grecian or Latin literature to compare with it. In Greek and Roman fables gods suffered for other gods, and yet none were surrounded with such absolutely mythical experiences as those through which the demi-god Maui of the Pacific Ocean passed when he entered the gates of death with the hope of winning immortality for mankind. The really remarkable group of legends which cluster around Maui is well concluded by the story of his unselfish and heroic battle with death.

The different islands of the Pacific have their Hades, or abode of dead. It is, with very few exceptions, down in the interior of the earth. Sometimes the tunnels left by currents of melted lava are the passages into the home of departed spirits. In Samoa there are two circular holes among the rocks at the west end of the island Savaii. These are the entrances to the under-world for chiefs and people. The spirits of those who die on the other islands leap into the sea and swim around the land from island to island until they reach Savaii. Then they plunge down into their heaven or their hades.

The Tongans had a spirit island for the home of the dead. They said that some natives once sailed far away in a canoe and found this island. It was covered with all manner of beautiful fruits, among which rare birds sported. They landed, but the trees were shadows. They grasped but could not hold them. The fruits and the birds were shadows. The men ate, but swallowed nothing substantial. It was shadow-land. They walked through all the delights their eyes looked upon, but found no substance. They returned home, but ever seemed to listen to spirits calling them back to the island. In a short time all the voyagers were dead.

There is no escape from death. The natives of New Zealand say: "Man may have descendants, but the daughters of the night strangle his offspring"; and again: "Men make heroes, but death carries them away."

There are very few legends among the Polynesians concerning the death of Maui. And these are usually fragmentary, except among the Maoris of New Zealand.

The Hawaiian legend of the death of Maui is to the effect that he offended some of the greater gods living in Waipio valley on the Island of Hawaii. Kanaloa, one of the four greatest gods of Hawaii, seized him and dashed him against the rocks. His blood burst from, the body and colored the earth red in the upper part of the valley. The Hawaiians in another legend say that Maui was chasing a boy and girl in Honolii gulch, Hawaii. The girl climbed a breadfruit tree. Maui changed himself into an eel and stretched himself along the side of the trunk of the tree. The tree stretched itself upward and Maui failed to reach the girl. A priest came along and struck the eel and killed it, and so Maui died. This is evidently a changed form of the legend of Maui and the long eel. Another Hawaiian fragment approaches very near to the beautiful New Zealand myth. The Hawaiians said that Maui attempted to tear a mountain apart. He wrenched a great hole in the side. Then the elepaio bird sang and the charm was broken. The cleft in the mountain could not be enlarged. If the story could be completed it would not be strange if the death of Maui came with this failure to open the path through the mountain.

The Hervey Islands say that after Maui fished up the islands his hook was thrown into the heavens and became the curved tail of the constellation of stars which we know as "The Scorpion." Then the people became angry with Maui and threw him up into the sky and his body is still thought to be hanging among the stars of the scorpion.

The Samoans, according to Turner, say that Maui went fishing and tried to catch the land under the seas and pull it to the surface. Finally an island appeared, but the people living on it were angry with Maui and drove him away into the heavens.

As he leaped from the island it separated into two parts. Thus the Samoans account for the origin of two of their islands and also for the passing away of Maui from the earth.

The natives of New Zealand have many myths concerning the death of Maui. Each tribe tells the story with such variations as would be expected when the fact is noted that these tribes have preserved their individuality through many generations. The substance of the myth, however, is the same.

In Maui's last days he longed for the victory over death. His innate love of life led him to face the possibility of escaping and overcoming the relentless enemy of mankind and thus bestow the boon of deathlessness upon his fellow-men. He had been successful over and over again in his contests with both gods and men. When man was created, he stood erect, but, according to an Hawaiian myth, had jointless arms and limbs. A web of skin connected and fastened tightly the arms to the body and the legs to each other. "Maui was angry at this motionless statue and took him and broke his legs at ankle, knee and hip and then, tearing them and the arms from the body, destroyed the web. Then he broke the arms at the elbow and shoulder. Then man could move from place to place, but he had neither fingers or toes." Here comes the most ancient Polynesian statement of the theory of evolution: "Hunger impelled man to seek his food in the mountains, where his toes were cut out by the brambles in climbing, and his fingers were also formed by the sharp splinters of the bamboo while searching with his arms for food in the ground."

It was not strange that Maui should feel self-confident when considering the struggle for immortality as a gift to be bestowed upon mankind. And yet his father warned him that his time of failure would surely come.

White, who has collected many of the myths and legends of New Zealand, states that after Maui had ill-treated Mahu-ika, his grandmother, the goddess and guardian of fire in the under-world, his father and mother tried to teach him to do differently. But he refused to listen. Then the father said:

"You heard our instructions, but please yourself and persist for life or death."

Maui replied: "What do I care? Do you think I shall cease? Rather I will persist forever and ever."

Then his father said: "There is one so powerful that no tricks can be of any avail."

Maui asked: "By what shall I be overcome?" The answer was that one of his ancestors, Hine-nui-te-po (Great Hine of the night), the guardian of life, would overcome him.

When Maui fished islands out of the deep seas, it was said that Hine made her home on the outer edge of one of the outermost islands. There the glow of the setting sun lighted the thatch of her house and covered it with glorious colors. There Great Hine herself stood flashing and sparkling on the edge of the horizon.

Maui, in these last days of his life, looked toward the west and said: "Let us investigate this matter and learn whether life or death shall follow."

The father replied: "There is evil hanging over you. When I chanted the invocation of your childhood, when you were made sacred and guarded by charms, I forgot a part of the ceremony. And for this you are to die."

Then Maui said, "Will this be by Hine-nui-te-po? What is she like?"

The father said that the flashing eyes they could see in the distance were dark as greenstone, the teeth were as sharp as volcanic glass, her mouth was large like a fish, and her hair was floating in the air like sea-weed.

One of the legends of New Zealand says that Maui and his brothers went toward the west, to the edge of the horizon, where they saw the goddess of the night. Light was flashing from her body. Here they found a great pit—the home of night. Maui entered the pit—telling his brothers not to laugh. He passed through and turning about started to return. The brothers laughed and the walls of night closed in around him and held him till he died.

The longer legend tells how Maui after his conversation with his father, remembered his conflict with the moon. He had tied her so that she could not escape, but was compelled to bathe in the waters of life and return night after night lest men should be in darkness when evening came.

Maui said to the goddess of the moon: "Let death be short. As the moon dies and returns with strength, so let men die and revive again."

But she replied: "Let death be very long, that man may sigh and sorrow. When man dies, let him go into darkness, become like earth, that those he leaves behind may weep and wail and mourn." according

Maui did not lay aside his purpose, but according to the New Zealand story, "did not wish men to die but to live forever. Death appeared degrading and an insult to the dignity of man. Man ought to die like the moon, which dips in the life-giving waters of Kane and is renewed again, or like the sun, which daily sinks into the pit of night and with renewed strength rises in the morning."

Maui sought the home of Hine-nui-te-po—the guardian of life. He heard her order her attendants to watch for any one approaching and capture all who came walking upright as a man. He crept past the attendants on hands and feet, found the place of life, stole some of the food of the goddess and returned home. He showed the food to his brothers and persuaded them to go with him into the darkness of the night of death. On the way he changed them into the form of birds. In the evening they came to the house of the goddess on the island long before fished up from the seas.

Maui warned the birds to refrain from making any noise -while he made the supreme effort of his life. He was about to enter upon his struggle for immortality. He said to the birds: "If I go into the stomach of this woman, do not laugh until I have gone through her, and come out again at her month; then you can laugh at me."

His friends said: "You will be killed." Maui replied: "If you laugh at me when I have only entered her stomach I shall be killed, but if I have passed through her and come out of her mouth I shall escape and Hine-nui-te-po will die."

His friends called out to him: "Go then. The decision is with you."

Hine was sleeping soundly. The flashes of lightning had all ceased. The sunlight had almost passed away and the house lay in quiet gloom. Maui came near to the sleeping goddess. Her large, fish-like mouth was open wide. He put off his clothing and prepared to pass through the ordeal of going to the hidden source of life, to tear it out of the body of its guardian and carry it back with him, to mankind. He stood in all the glory of savage manhood. His body was splendidly marked by the tattoo-bones, and now well oiled shone and sparkled in the last rays of the setting sun.

He leaped through the mouth of the enchanted one and entered her stomach, weapon in band, to take out her heart, the vital principle which he knew had its home somewhere within her being. He found immortality on the other side of death. He turned to come back again into life when suddenly a little bird (the Pata-tai) laughed in a clear, shrill tone, and Great Hine, through whose mouth Maui was passing, awoke. Her sharp, obsidian teeth closed with a snap upon Maui, cutting his body in the center. Thus Maui entered the gates of death, but was unable to return, and death has ever since been victor over rebellious men. The natives have the saying:

"If Maui had not died, he could have restored to life all who had gone before him, and thus succeeded in destroying death."

Maui's brothers took the dismembered body and buried it in a cave called Te-ana-i-hana, "The cave dug out," possibly a prepared burial place.

Maui's wife made war upon the spirits, the gods, and killed as many as she could to avenge her husband's death. One of the old native poets of New Zealand, in chanting the story to Mr. White, said: "But though Maui was killed, his offspring survived. Some of these are at Hawa-i-i-ki and some at Aotearoa (New Zealand), but the greater part of them remained at Hawa-i-ki. This history was handed down by the generations of our ancestors of ancient times, and we continue to rehearse it to our children, with our incantations and genealogies, and all other matters relating to our race."

> *"But death is nothing new,*
> *Death is, and has been ever since old Maui died.*
> *Then Pata-tai laughed loud*
> *And woke the goblin-god,*
> *Who severed him in two, and shut him in,*
> *So dusk of eve came on."*

—Maori death chant, New Zealand

XII

HINA OF HILO

Hina is not an uncommon name in Hawaiian genealogies. It is usually accompanied by some adjective which explains or identifies the person to whom the name is given. In Hawaii the name Hina is feminine. This is also true throughout all Polynesia except in a few cases where Hina is reckoned as a man with supernatural attributes. Even in these cases it is apparent that the legend has been changed from its original form as it has been carried to small islands by comparatively ignorant people when moving away from their former homes.

Hina is a Polynesian goddess whose story is very interesting—one worthy of study when comparing the legends of the island groups of the Pacific. The Hina of Hilo is the same as the goddess of that name most widely known throughout Polynesia—and yet her legends are located by the ancient Hawaiians in Hilo, as if that place were her only home. The legends are so old that the Hawaiians have forgotten their origin in other lands. The stories were brought with the immigrants who settled on the Hilo coast. Thus the stories found their final location with the families who brought them. There are three Hawaiian Hinas practically distinct from each other, although a supernatural element is connected with each one. Hina who was stolen from Hawaii by a chief of the Island of Molokai was an historical character, although surrounded by mythical stories. Another Hina, who was the wife of Kuula, the fish god, was pre-eminently a local deity, having no real connection with the legends of the other islands of the Pacific, although sometimes the stories told concerning her have not been kept entirely distinct from the legends of the Hina of Hilo.

The Hilo Hina was the true legendary character closely connected with all Polynesia. The stories about her are of value not simply as legends, but as traditions closely uniting the Hawaiian Islands with the island groups thousands of miles distant. The Wailuku river, which flows through the town of Hilo, has its own peculiar and weird beauty. For miles it is a series of waterfalls and rapids. It follows the course of an ancient lava flow, sometimes forcing its way under bridges of lava, thus forming what are called boiling pots, and sometimes pouring in massive sheets over the edges of precipices which never disintegrate. By the side of this river Hina's son, Maui had his lands. In the very bed of the river, in a cave under one of the largest falls, Hina made her own home, concealed from the world by the silver veil of falling water and lulled to sleep by the continual roar of the flood falling into the deep pool below. By the side of this river, the legends say, she pounded her tapa and prepared her food. Here were the small, graceful mamake and the coarser wauke trees, from which the bark was stripped with which she made tapa cloth. Branches were cut or broken from these and other trees whose bark was fit for the purpose. These branches were well soaked until the bark was removed easily. Then the outer bark was scraped off, leaving only the pliable inner bark. The days were very short and there was no time for rest while making tapa cloth. Therefore, as soon as the morning light reddened the clouds, Hina would take her calabash filled with water to pour upon the bark, and her little bundle of round clubs (the hohoa) and her four-sided mallets (the i-e-kuku) and hasten to the sacred spot where, with chants and incantations, the tapa was made.

The bark was well soaked in the water all the days of the process of tapa making. Hina took small bundles of the wet inner bark and laid them on the kua or heavy tapa board, pounding them together into a pulpy mass with her round clubs. Then using the four-sided mallets, she beat this pulp into thin sheets. Beautiful tapa, soft as silk, was made by adding pulpy mass to pulpy mass and beating it day after day until the fibres were lost and a sheet of close-woven bark cloth was formed. Although Hina was a goddess and had a family possessing miraculous power, it never entered the mind of the Hawaiian legend tellers to endow her with case in producing wonderful results. The legends of the Southern Pacific Islands show more imagination. They say that Ina (Hina) was such a wonderful artist in making beautiful tapas that she was placed in the skies, where she beat out glistening fine tapas, the white and glorious clouds. When she stretches these clouds sheets out to dry, she places stones along the edges, so that the fierce winds of the heavens shall not blow them away. When she throws these stones aside, the skies reverberate with thunder. When she rolls her cloud sheets of tapa together, the folds glisten with flashes of light and lightning leaps from sheet to sheet.

The Hina of Hilo was grieved as she toiled because after she had pounded the sheets out so thin that they were ready to be dried, she found it almost impossible to secure the necessary aid of the sun in the drying process. She would rise as soon as she could see and hasten to spread out the tapa made the day before. But the sun always hurried so fast that the sheets could not dry. He leaped from the ocean waters in the earth, rushed across the heavens and plunged into the dark waters again on the other side of the island before she could even turn her tapas so that they might dry evenly. This legend of very short days is strange because of its place not only among the myths of Hawaii but also because it belongs to practically all the tropical islands of the Pacific Ocean. In Tahiti the legends said that the sun rushed across the sky very rapidly. The days were too short for fruits to ripen or for work to be finished. In Samoa the "mats" made by Sina had no time to dry. The ancestors of the Polynesians sometime somewhere must have been in the region of short days and long nights. Hina found that her incantations had no influence with the sun. She could not prevail upon him to go slower and give her more time for the completion of her task. Then she called on her powerful son, Maui-ki-i-ki-i, for aid.

Some of the legends of the Island Maui say that Hina dwelt by the sea coast of that island near the high hill Kauwiki at the foot of the great mountain Haleakala, House of the Sun, and that there, facing the southern skies under the most favorable conditions for making tapa, she found the days too short for the tapa to dry. At the present time the Hawaiians point out a long, narrow stone not far from the surf and almost below the caves in which the great queen Kaahumanu spent the earliest days of her childhood.

This stone is said to be the kua or tapa board on which Hina pounded the bark for her cloth. Other legends of that same island locate Hina's home on the northeast coast near Pohakuloa.

The Hilo legends, however, do not deem it necessary that Hina and Maui should have their home across the wide channel which divides the Island Hawaii from the Island Maui in order to wage war successfully with the inconsiderate sun. Hina remained in her home by the Wailuku river, sometimes resting in her cave under Rainbow Falls, and sometimes working on the river bank, trusting her powerful son Maui to make the swiftly-passing lord of day go more slowly.

Maui possessed many supernatural powers. He could assume the form of birds or insects. He could call on the winds to do his will, or he could, if he wished, traverse miles with a single stride. It is interesting to note that the Hilo legends differ as to the way in which Ma-ui the man passed over to Mau-i the island. One legend says that he crossed the channel, miles wide, with a single step. Another says that he launched his canoe and with a breath the god of the winds placed him on the opposite coast, while another story says that Maui assumed the form of a white chicken, which flew over the waters to Haleakala. Here he took ropes made from the fibre of trees and vines and lassoed the sun while it climbed the side of the mountain and entered the great crater which hollows out the summit. The sun came through a large gap in the eastern side of the crater, rushing along as rapidly as possible. Then Maui threw his lassoes one after the other over the sun's legs (the rays of light), holding him fast and breaking off some of them. With a magic club Maui struck the face of the sun again and again. At last, wounded and weary, and also limping on its broken legs, the sun promised Maui to go slowly forevermore.

"La" among the Polynesians, like the word "Ra" among the Egyptians, means "sun" or "day" or "sun-god"—and the mountain where the son of Hina won his victory over the monster of the heavens has long borne the name Hale-a-ka-la, or House of the Sun.

Hina of Hilo soon realized the wonderful deed which Maui had done. She spread out her fine tapas with songs of joy and cheerily performed the task which filled the hours of the day. The comfort of sunshine and cooling winds came with great power into Hina's life, bringing to her renewed joy and beauty.

XIII

Hina and the Wailuku River

Here are two rivers of rushing, tumbling rapids and waterfalls in the Hawaiian Islands, both bearing the name of Wailuku. One is on the Island of Maui, flowing out of a deep gorge in the side of the extinct volcano Iao. Yosemite-like precipices surround this majestically-walled crater. The name Iao means "asking for clouds." The head of the crater-valley is almost always covered with great masses of heavy rain clouds. Out of the crater the massed waters rush in a swift-flowing stream, of only four or five miles, emptying into Kahului harbor. The other Wailuku river is on the Island of Hawaii. The snows melt on the summits of the two great mountains, Mauna Kea and Mauna Loa. The water seeps through the porous lava from the eastern slope of Mauna Loa and the southern slope of Mauna Kea, meeting where the lava flows of centuries from each mountain have piled up against each other. Through the fragments of these volcanic battles the waters creep down the mountain side toward the sea.

At one place, a number of miles above the city of Hilo, the waters were heard gurgling and splashing far below the surface. Water was needed for the sugar plantations, which modern energy has established all along the eastern coast of the large island. A tunnel was cut into the lava, the underground stream was tapped—and an abundant supply of water secured and sluiced down to the large plantations below. The head waters of the Wailuku river gathered from the melting snow of the mountains found these channels, which centered at last in the bed of a very ancient and very interesting lava flow. Sometimes breaking forth in a large, turbulent flood, the stream forces its way over and around the huge blocks of lava which mark the course of the eruption of long ago. Sometimes it courses in a tunnel left by the flowing lava and comes up from below in a series of boiling pools. Then again it falls in majestic sheets over high walls of worn precipices. Several large falls and some very picturesque smaller cascades interspersed with rapids and natural bridges give to, this river a beauty peculiarly its own. The most weird of all the rough places through which the Wailuku river flows is that known as the basin of Rainbow Falls near Hilo. Here Hina, the moon goddess of the Polynesians, lived in a great open cave, over which the falls hung their misty, rainbow-tinted veil. Her son Maui, the mighty demi-god of Polynesia, supposed by some writers to be the sun-god of the Polynesians, had extensive lands along the northern bank of the river. Here among his cultivated fields he had his home, from which he went forth to accomplish the wonders attributed to him in the legends of the Hawaiians.

Below the cave in which Hina dwelt the river fought its way through a narrow gorge and then, in a series of many sinall falls, descended to the little bay, where its waters mingled with the surf of the salt sea. Far above the cave, in the bed of the river, dwelt Kuna. The district through which that portion of the river runs bears to this day the name "Wai-kuna" or "Kuna's river." When the writer was talking with the natives concerning this part of the old legend, they said "Kuna is not a Hawaiian word. It means something like a snake or a dragon, something we do not have in these islands." This, they thought, made the connection with the Hina legend valueless until they were shown that Tuna (or kuna) was the New Zealand name of a reptile which attacked Hina and struck her with his tail like a crocodile, for which Maui killed him. When this was understood, the Hawaiians were greatly interested to give the remainder of this legend and compare it with the New Zealand story. In New Zealand there are several statements concerning Tuna's dwelling place. He is sometimes represented as coming from a pool to attack Hina and sometimes from a distant stream, and sometimes from the river by which Hina dwelt. The Hawaiians told of the annoyances which Hina endured from Kuna while he lived above her home in the Wailuku. He would stop up the river and fill it with dirt as when the freshets brought down the debris of the storms from the mountain sides. He would throw logs and rolling stones into the stream that they might be carried over the falls and drive Hina from her cave. He had sought Hina in many ways and had been repulsed again and again until at last hatred took the place of all more kindly feelings and he determined to destroy the divine chiefess.

Hina was frequently left with but little protection, and yet from her home in the cave feared nothing that Kuna could do. Precipices guarded the cave on either side, and any approach of an enemy through the falling water could be easily thwarted. So her chants rang out through the river valley even while floods swirled around her, and Kuna's missiles were falling over the rocky bed of the stream toward her.

Kuna became very angry and, tittering great curses and calling upon all his magic forces to aid him, caught a great stone and at night hurled it into the gorge of the river below Hina's home, filling the river bed from bank to bank. "Ah, Hina! Now is the danger, for the river rises. The water cannot flow away. Awake! Awake!"

Hina is not aware of this evil which is so near. The water rises and rises, higher and higher. "Auwe! Auwe! Alas, alas, Hina must perish!" The water entered the opening of the cave and began to creep along the floor. Hina cannot fly, except into the very arms of her great enemy, who is waiting to destroy her. Then Hina called for Maui. Again and again her voice went out from the cave. It pierced through the storms and the clouds which attended Kuna's attack upon her. It swept along the side of the great mountain. It crossed the channel between the islands of Hawaii and Maui. Its anguish smote the side of the great mountain Haleakala, where Maui had been throwing his lassoes around the sun and compelling him, to go more slowly. When Maui heard Hina's cry for help echoing from cliff to cliff and through the ravines, he leaped at once to rush to her assistance.

Some say that Hina, the goddess, had a cloud servant, the "ao-opua," the "warning cloud," which rose swiftly above the falls when Hina cried for aid and then, assuming a peculiar shape, stood high above the hills that Maui might see it. Down the mountain he leaped to his magic canoe. Pushing it into the sea with two mighty strokes of his paddle lie crossed the sea to the mouth of the Wailuku river. Here even to the present day lies a long double rock, surrounded by the waters of the bay, which the natives call Ka waa o Maui, "The canoe of Maui." It represents to Hawaiian thought the magic canoe with which Maui always sailed over the ocean more swiftly than any winds could carry him. Leaving his canoe, Maui seized the magic club with which he had conquered the sun after lassoing him, and rushed along the dry bed of the river to the place of danger. Swinging the club swiftly around his head, lie struck the dam holding back the water of the rapidly-rising river.

"Ah! Nothing can withstand the magic club. The bank around one end of the dam gives way. The imprisoned waters leap into the new channel. Safe is Hina the goddess."

Kuna heard the crash of the club against the stones of the river bank and fled up the river to his home in the hidden caves by the pools in the river bed. Maui rushed up the river to punish Kuna-mo-o for the trouble he had caused Hina. When he came to the place where the dragon was hidden under deep waters, he took his magic spear and thrust it through the dirt and lava rocks along one side of the river, making a long hole, through which the waters rushed, revealing Kuna-mo-o's hiding place. This place of the spear thrust is known among the Hawaiians as Ka puka a Maui, "the door made by Maui." It is also known as "The natural bridge of the Wailuku river."

Kuna-mo-o fled to his different hiding places, but Maui broke up the river bed and drove the dragon out from every one, following him from place to place as he fled down the river. Apparently this is a legendary account of earthquakes. At last Kuna-mo-o found what seemed to be a safe hiding place in a series of deep pools, but Maui poured a lava flow into the river. He threw red-hot burning stones into the water until the pools were boiling and the steam was rising in clouds. Kuna uttered incantation after incantation, but the water scalded and burned him. Dragon as he was, his hard, tough skin was of no avail. The pain was becoming unbearable. With cries to his gods he leaped from the pools and fled down the river. The waters of the pools are no longer scalding, but they have never lost the tumbling, tossing, foaming, boiling swirl which Maui gave to them when he threw into them the red-hot stones with which he hoped to destroy Kuna, and they are known today as "The Boiling Pots."

Some versions of the legend say that Maui poured boiling water in the river and sent it in swift pursuit of Kuna, driving him froin point to point and scalding his life out of him. Others say that Maui chased the dragon, striking him again and again with his consecrated weapons, following Kuna down from falls to falls until he came to the place where Hina dwelt. Then, feeling that there was little use in flight, Kuna battled with Maui. His struggles were of no avail. He was forced over the falls into the stream below. Hina and her women encouraged Maui by their chants and strengthened him by the most powerful incantations with which they were acquainted. Great was their joy when they beheld Kuna's ponderous body hurled over the falls. Eagerly they watched the dragon as the swift waters swept him against the dam with which he had hoped to destroy Hina; and when the whirling waves caught him and dashed him through the new channel made by Maui's magic club, they rejoiced and sang the praise of the mighty warrior who had saved them. Maui had rushed along the bank of the river with tremendous strides overtaking the dragon as he was rolled over and over among the small waterfalls near the mouth of the river. Here Matii again attacked Kuna, at last beating the life out of his body. "Moo-Kuna" was the name given by the Hawaiians to the dragon. "Moo" means anything in lizard shape, but Kuna was unlike any lizard known in the Hawaiian Islands. Moo Kuna is the name sometimes given to a long black stone lying like an island in the waters between the small falls of the river. As one who calls attention to this legendary black stone says: "As if he were not dead enough already, every big freshet in the stream beats him and pounds him and drowns him over and over as he would have drowned Hina." A New Zealand legend relates a conflict of incantations, somewhat like the filling in of the Wailuku river by Kuna, and the cleaving of a new channel by Maui with the different use of means. In New Zealand the river is closed by the use of powerful incantations and charms and reopened by the use of those more powerful.

In the Hervey Islands, Tuna, the god of eels, loved Ina (Hina) and finally died for her, giving his head to be buried. From, this head sprang two cocoanut trees, bearing fruit marked with Tuna's eyes and mouth.

In Samoa the battle was between an owl and a serpent. The owl conquered by calling in the aid of a friend.

This story of Hina apparently goes far back in the traditions of Polynesians, even to their ancient home in Hawaiki, from which it was taken by one branch of the family to New Zealand and by another to the Hawaiian Islands and other groups in the Pacific Ocean. The dragon may even be a remembrance of the days when the Polynesians were supposed to dwell by the banks of the River Ganges in India, when crocodiles were dangerous enemies and heroes saved families from their destructive depredations.

XIV

Ghosts of the Hilo Hills

The legends about Hina and her famous son Maui and her less widely known daughters are common property among the natives of the beautiful little city of Hilo. One of these legends of more than ordinary interest finds its location in the three small hills back of Hilo toward the mountains.

These hills are small craters connected with some ancient lava flow of unusual violence. The eruption must have started far up on the slopes of Mauna Loa. As it sped down toward the sea it met some obstruction which, although overwhelmed, checked the flow and caused a great mass of cinders and ashes to be thrown out until a large hill with a hollow crater was built up, covering many acres of ground.

Soon the lava found another vent and then another obstruction and a second and then a third hill were formed nearer the sea. These hills or extinct craters bear the names Halai, Opeapea and Puu Honu. They are not far from the Wailuku river, famous for its picturesque waterfalls and also for the legends which are told along its banks. Here Maui had his lands overlooking the steep bluffs. Here in a cave under the Rainbow Falls was the home of Hina, the mother of Maui, according to the Hawaiian stories. Other parts of the Pacific sometimes make Hina Maui's wife, and sometimes a goddess from whom he descended. In the South Sea legends Hina was thought to have married the moon. Her home was in the skies, where she wove beautiful tapa cloths (the clouds), which were bright and glistening, so that when she rolled them up flashes of light (cloud lightning) could be seen on the earth. She laid heavy stones on the corners of these tapas, but sometimes the stones rolled off and made the thunder. Hina of the Rainbow Falls was a famous tapa maker whose tapa was the cause of Maui's conflict with the sun.

Hina had several daughters, four of whose names are given: Hina Ke Ahi, Hina Ke Kai, Hina Mahuia, and Hina Kuluua. Each name marked the peculiar "mana" or divine gift which Hina, the mother, had bestowed upon her daughters.

Hina Ke Ahi meant the Hina who had control of fire. This name is sometimes given to Hina the mother. Hina Ke Kai was the daughter who had power over the sea. She was said to have been in a canoe with her brother Maui when he fished up Cocoanut Island, his line breaking before he could pull it up to the mainland and make it fast. Hina Kuluua was the mistress over the forces of rain. The winds and the storms were supposed to obey her will. Hina Mahuia is peculiarly a name connected with the legends of the other island groups of the Pacific. Mahuia or Mafuie was a god or goddess of fire all through Polynesia.

The legend of the Hilo hills pertains especially to Hina Ke Ahi and Hina Kuluua. Hina the mother gave the hill Halai to Hina Ke Ahi and the hill Puu Honu to Hina Kuluua for their families and dependents.

The hills were of rich soil and there was much rain. Therefore, for a long time, the two daughters had plenty of food for themselves and their people, but at last the days were like fire and the sky had no rain in it. The taro planted on the hillsides died. The bananas and sugar cane and sweet potatoes withered and the fruit on the trees was blasted. The people were faint because of hunger, and the shadow of death was over the land. Hina Ke Ahi pitied her suffering friends and determined to provide food for them. Slowly her people labored at her command. Over they went to the banks of the river course, which was only the bed of an ancient lava stream, over which no water was flowing; the famished laborers toiled, gathering and carrying back whatever wood they could find, then up the mountain side to the great koa and ohia forests, gathering their burdens of fuel according to the wishes of their chiefess.

Their sorcerers planted charms along the way and uttered incantations to ward off the danger of failure. The priests offered sacrifices and prayers for the safe and successful return of the burden-bearers. After many days the great quantity of wood desired by the goddess was piled up by the side of the Halai Hill.

Then came the days of digging out the hill and making a great imu or cooking oven and preparing it with stones and wood. Large quantities of wood were thrown into the place. Stones best fitted for retaining heat were gathered and the fires kindled. When the stones were hot, Hina Ke Ahi directed the people to arrange the imu in its proper order for cooking the materials for a great feast. A place was made for sweet potatoes, another for taro, another for pigs and another for dogs. All the form of preparing the food for cooking was passed through, but no real food was laid on the stones. Then Hina told them to make a place in the imu for a human sacrifice. Probably out of every imu of the long ago a small part of the food was offered to the gods, and there may have been a special place in the imu for that part of the food to be cooked. At any rate Hina had this oven so built that the people understood that a remarkable sacrifice would be offered in it to the gods, who for some reason had sent the famine upon the people.

Human sacrifices were frequently offered by the Hawaiians even after the days of the coming of Captain Cook. A dead body was supposed to be acceptable to the gods when a chief's house was built, when a chief's new canoe was to be made or when temple walls were to be erected or victories celebrated. The bodies of the people belonged to the will of the chief. Therefore it was in quiet despair that the workmen obeyed Hina Ke Ahi and prepared the place for sacrifice. It might mean their own holocaust as an offering to the gods. At last Hina Ke Ahi bade the laborers cease their work and stand by the side of the oven ready to cover it with the dirt which had been thrown out and piled up by the side. The people stood by, not knowing upon whom, the blow might fall.

But Hina Ke Ahi was "Hina the kind," and although she stood before them robed in royal majesty and power, still her face was full of pity and love. Her voice melted the hearts of her retainers as she bade them carefully follow her directions.

"O my people. Where are you? Will you obey and do as I command? This imu is my imu. I shall lie down on its bed of burning stones. I shall sleep under its cover. But deeply cover ine or I may perish. Quickly throw the dirt over in), body. Fear not the fire. Watch for three days. A woman will stand by the imu. Obey her will."

Hina Ke Ahi was very beautiful, and her eyes flashed light like fire as she stepped into the great pit and lay down on the burning stones. A great smoke arose and gathered over the imu. The men toiled rapidly, placing the imu mats over their chiefess and throwing the dirt back into the oven until it was all thoroughly covered and the smoke was quenched.

Then they waited for the strange, mysterious thing which must follow the sacrifice of this divine chiefess.

Halai hill trembled and earthquakes shook the land round about. The great heat of the fire in the imu withered the little life which was still left from the famine. Meanwhile Hina Ke Ahi was carrying out her plan for securing aid for her people. She could not be injured by the heat for she was a goddess of fire. The waves of heat raged around her as she sank down through the stones of the imu into the underground paths which belonged to the spirit world. The legend says that Hina made her appearance in the form of a gushing stream of water which would always supply the want of her adherents. The second day passed. Hina was still journeying underground, but this time she came to the surface as a pool named Moe Waa (canoe sleep) much nearer the sea. The third day came and Hina caused a great spring of sweet water to burst forth from the sea shore in the very path of the ocean surf. This received the name Auauwai. Here Hina washed away all traces of her journey through the depths. This was the last of the series of earthquakes and the appearance of new water springs. The people waited, feeling that some more wonderful event must follow the remarkable experiences of the three days. Soon a woman stood by the imu, who commanded the laborers to dig away the dirt and remove the mats. When this was done, the hungry people found a very great abundance of food, enough to supply their want until the food plants should have time to ripen and the days of the famine should be over.

The joy of the people was great when they knew that their chiefess had escaped death and would still dwell among them in comfort. Many were the songs sung and stories told about the great famine and the success of the goddess of fire.

The second sister, Hina Kuluua, the goddess of rain, was always very jealous of her beautiful sister Hina Ke Ahi, and many times sent rain to put out fires which her sister tried to kindle. Hina Ke Ahi could not stand the rain and so fled with her people to a home by the seaside.

Hina Kuluua (or Hina Kuliua as she was sometimes known among the Hawaiians) could control rain and storms, but for some reason failed to provide a food supply for her people, and the famine wrought havoc among them. She thought of the stories told and songs sung about her sister and wished for the same honor for herself. She commanded her people to make a great imu for her in the hill Pun Honu. She knew that a strange power belonged to her and yet, blinded by jealousy, forgot that rain and fire could not work together. She planned to furnish a great supply of food for her people in the same way in which her sister had worked.

The oven was dug. Stones and wood were collected and the same ghostly array of potatoes, taro, pig and dog prepared as had been done before by her sister.

The kahunas or priests knew that Hina Kuluua was going out of her province in trying to do as her sister had done, but there was no use in attempting to change her plans. jealousy is self-willed and obstinate and no amount of reasoning from her dependents could have any influence over her.

The ordinary incantations were observed, and Hina Kulutia gave the same directions as those her sister had given. The imu was to be well heated. The make-believe food was to be put in and a place left for her body. It was the goddess of rain making ready to lie down on a bed prepared for the goddess of fire. When all was ready, she lay down on the heated stones and the oven mats were thrown over her and the ghostly provisions. Then the covering of dirt was thrown back upon the mats and heated stones, filling the pit which had been dug. The goddess of rain was left to prepare a feast for her people as the goddess of fire had done for herfollowers.

Some of the legends have introduced the demi-god Maui into this story. The natives say that Maui came to "burn" or "cook the rain" and that he made the oven very hot, but that the goddess of rain escaped and hung over the hill in the form of a cloud. At least this is what the people saw—not a cloud of smoke over the imu, but a rain cloud. They waited and watched for such evidences of underground labor as attended the passage of Hina Ke Ahi through the earth from the hill to the sea, but the only strange appearance was the dark rain cloud. They waited three days and looked for their chiefess to come in the form of a woman. They waited another day and still another and no signs or wonders were manifest. Meanwhile Maui, changing himself into a white bird, flew up into the sky to catch the ghost of the goddess of rain which had escaped from the burning oven. Having caught this spirit, he rolled it in some kapa cloth which lie kept for food to be placed in an oven and carried it to a place in the forest on the mountain side where again the attempt was made to "burn the rain," but a great drop escaped and sped upward into the sky. Again Maui can ht the ghost of the goddess and carried it to a pali or precipice below the great volcano Kilauea, where he again tried to destroy it in the heat of a great lava oven, but this time the spirit escaped and found a safe refuge among kukui trees on the mountain side, from which she sometimes rises in clouds which the natives say are the sure sign of rain.

Whether this Maui legend has any real connection with the two Hinas and the famine we do not surely know. The legend ordinarily told among the Hawaiians says that after five days had passed the retainers decided on their own responsibility to open the imu. No woman had appeared to give them directions. Nothing but a mysterious rain cloud over the hill. In doubt and fear, the dirt was thrown off and the mats removed. Nothing was found but the ashes of Hina Kuluua. There was no food for her followers and the goddess had lost all power of appearing as a chiefess. Her bitter and thoughtless jealousy brought destruction upon herself and her people. The ghosts of Hina Ke Ahi and Hina Kuluua sometimes draw near to the old hills in the form of the fire of flowing lava or clouds of rain while the old men and women tell the story of the Hinas, the sisters of Maui, who were laid upon the burning stones of the imus of a famine.

XV

HINA, THE WOMAN IN THE MOON

The Wailuku river has by its banks far up the mountain side some of the most ancient of the various interesting picture rocks of the Hawaiian Islands. The origin of the Hawaiian picture writing is a problem still unsolved, but the picture rocks of the Wailuku river are called "na kii o Maui," "the Maui pictures." Their antiquity is beyond question.

The most prominent figure cut in these rocks is that of the crescent moon. The Hawaiian legends do not attempt any direct explanation of the meaning of this picture writing. The traditions of the Polynesians both concerning Hina and Matti look to Hina as the moon goddess of their ancestors, and in some measure the Hawaiian stories confirm the traditions of the other island groups of the Pacific.

Fornander, in his history of the Polynesian race, gives the Hawaiian story of Hina's ascent to the moon, but applies it to a Hina the wife of a chief called Aikanaka rather than to the Hina of Hilo, the wife of Akalana, the father of Maui. However, Fornander evidently found some difficulty in determining the status of the one to whom he refers the legend, for he calls her "the mysterious wife of Aikanaka." In some of the Hawaiian legends Hina, the mother of Maui, lived on the southeast coast of the Island Maui at the foot of a hill famous in Hawaiian story as Kauiki. Fornander says that this "mysterious wife" of Aikanaka bore her children Puna and Huna, the latter a noted sea-rover among the Polynesians, at the foot of this hill Kauiki. It can very easily be supposed that a legend of the Ilina connected with the demi-god Maui might be given during the course of centuries to the other Hina, the mother of Huna. The application of the legend would make no difference to anyone were it not for the fact that the story of Hina and her ascent to the moon has been handed down in different forms among the traditions of Samoa, New Zealand, Tonga, Hervey Islands, Fate Islands, Nauru and other Pacific island groups. The Polynesian name of the moon, Mahina or Masina, is derived from Hina, the goddess mother of Matii. It is even possible to trace the name back to "Sin," the moon god of the Assyrians.

The moon goddess of Ponape was Ina-inaram. (Hawaiian Hina-malamalama), "Hina giving light."

In the Paumotan Islands an eclipse of the sun is called Higa-higa-hana (Hina-hiua-hana), "The act (hana) of Hina—the moon."

In New Zealand moonless nights were called "Dark Hina."

In Tahiti it is said there was war among the gods. They cursed the stars. Hina saved them, although they lost a little light. Then they cursed the sea, but Hina preserved the tides. They cursed the rivers, but Hina saved the springs—the moving waters inland, like the tides in the ocean.

The Hawaiians say that Hina and her maidens pounded out the softest, finest kapa cloth on the long, thick kapa board at the foot of Kauiki. Incessantly the restless sea dashed its spray over the picturesque groups of splintered lava rocks which form the Kauiki headland. Here above the reach of the surf still lies the long, black stone into which the legends say Hina's kapa board was changed. Here Hina took the leaves of the hala tree and, after the manner of the Hawaiian women of the ages past, braided mats for the household to sleep upon, and from the nuts of the kukui trees fashioned the torches which were burned around the homes of those of high chief rank.

At last she became weary of her work among mortals. Her family had become more and more troublesome. It was said that her sons were unruly and her husband lazy and shiftless. She looked into the heavens and determined to flee up the pathway of her rainbow through the clouds.

The Sun was very bright and Hina said, "I will go to the Sun." So she left her home very early in the morning and climbed up, higher, higher, until the heat of the rays of the sun beat strongly upon her and weakened her so that she could scarcely crawl along her beautiful path. Up a little higher and the clouds no longer gave her even the least shadow. The heat from the sun was so great that she began to feel the fire shriveling and torturing her. Quickly she slipped down into the storms around her rainbow and then back to earth. As the day passed her strength came back, and when the full moon rose through the shadows of the night she said, "I will climb to the moon and there find rest."

But when Hina began to go upward her husband saw her and called to her: "Do not go into the heavens." She answered him: "My mind is fixed; I will go to my new husband, the moon." And she climbed up higher and higher. Her husband ran toward her. She was almost out of reach, but he leaped and caught her foot. This did not deter Hina from her purpose. She shook off her husband, but as he fell he broke her leg so that the lower part came off in his hands. Hina went up through the stars, crying out the strongest incantations she could use. The powers of the night aided her. The mysterious hands of darkness lifted her, until she stood at the door of the moon. She had packed her calabash with her most priceless possessions and had carried it with her even when injured by her cruel husband. With her calabash she limped into the moon and found her abiding home. When the moon is full, the Hawaiians of the long ago, aye and even today, look into the quiet, silvery light and see the goddess in her celestial home, her calabash by her side.

The natives call her now Lono-moku, "the crippled Lono." From this watch tower in the heavens she pointed out to Kahai, one of her descendents, the way to rise up into the skies. The ancient chant thus describes his ascent:

> *"The rainbow is the path of Kahai.*
> *Kahai rose. Kahai bestirred himself.*
> *Kahai passed on the floating cloud of Kane.*
> *Perplexed were the eyes of Alihi.*
> *Kahai passed on on the glancing light.*
> *The glancing light on men and canoes.*
> *Above was Hanaiakamalama." (Hina).*

Thus under the care of his ancestress Hina, Kahai, the great sea-rover, made his ascent in quest of adventures among the immortals.

In the Tongan Islands the legends say that Hina remains in the moon watching over the "fire-walkers" as their great protecting goddess.

The Hervey Island traditions say that the Moon (Marama) had often seen Hina and admired her, and at last had come down and caught her up to live with himself. The moonlight in its glory is called Inamotea, "the brightness of Ina."

The story as told on Atiu Island (one of the Society group) is that Hina took her human husband with her to the moon, where they dwelt happily for a time, but as he grew old she prepared a rainbow, down which he descended to the earth to die, leaving Hina forevermore as "the woman in the moon." The Savage Islanders worshiped the spirits of their ancestors, saying that many of them went up to the land of

Sina, the always bright land in the skies. To the natives of Niue Island, Hina has been the goddess ruling over all tapa making. They say that her home is "Motu a Hina," "the island of Hina," the home of the dead in the skies.

The Samoans said that the Moon received Hina and a child, and also her tapa board and mallet and material for the manufacture of tapa cloth. Therefore, when the moon is shining in full splendor, they shade their eyes and look for the goddess and the tools with which she fashions the tapa clouds in the heavens.

The New Zealand legend says that the woman went after water in the night. As she passed down the path to the spring the bright light of the full moon made the way easy for her quick footsteps, but when she had filled her calabash and started homeward, suddenly the bright light was hidden by a passing cloud and she stumbled against a stone in the path and fell to the ground, spilling the water she was carrying. Then she became very angry and cursed the moon heartily. Then the moon became angry and swiftly swept down upon her from the skies, grasping her and lifting her up. In her terrible fight she caught a small tree with one hand and her calabash with the other. But oh! the strong moon pulled her up with the tree and the calabash and there in the full m,oon they can all be traced when the nights are clear.

Pleasant or Nauru Island, in which a missionary from Central Union Church, Honolulu, is laboring, tells the story of Gigu, a beautiful young woman, who has many of the experiences of Hina. She opened the eyes of the Mother of the Moon as Hina, in some of the Polynesian legends, is represented to have opened the eyes of one of the great goddesses, and in reward is married to Maraman, the Moon, with whom she lives ever after, and in whose embrace she can always be seen when the moon is full. Gigu is Hina under another and more guttural form of speech. Maraman is the same as Malama, one of the Polynesian names for the moon.

A Note About the Author

W.D. Westervelt (1849–1939) was an American minister, historian, and folklorist specializing in Hawaiian mythology. Born in Oberlin, Ohio, he obtained his B.A. from Oberlin College before completing his B.D. from Oberlin Theological Seminary in 1874. In 1899, after serving as a pastor in Ohio and Colorado, Westervelt settled in Hawaii, where he married Caroline Dickinson Castle. A member of the Hawaiian Historical Society, he served as secretary, treasurer, and president, gaining a reputation as a leading scholar of Hawaiian folklore. Throughout his career, he wrote numerous articles and several anthologies on Hawaiian myths and legends, which continue to be recognized as some of the most reliable sources on the subject written in English.

A Note from the Publisher

Spanning many genres, from non-fiction essays to literature classics to children's books and lyric poetry, Mint Edition books showcase the master works of our time in a modern new package. The text is freshly typeset, is clean and easy to read, and features a new note about the author in each volume. Many books also include exclusive new introductory material. Every book boasts a striking new cover, which makes it as appropriate for collecting as it is for gift giving. Mint Edition books are only printed when a reader orders them, so natural resources are not wasted. We're proud that our books are never manufactured in excess and exist only in the exact quantity they need to be read and enjoyed. To learn more and view our library, go to minteditionbooks.com

bookfinity & MINT EDITIONS

Enjoy more of your favorite classics with Bookfinity,
a new search and discovery experience for readers.
With Bookfinity, you can discover more vintage
literature for your collection, find your Reader Type,
track books you've read or want to read,
and add reviews to your favorite books.
Visit www.bookfinity.com, and click on
Take the Quiz to get started.

Don't forget to follow us
@bookfinityofficial and @mint_editions

CPSIA information can be obtained
at www.ICGtesting.com
Printed in the USA
JSHW040937160822
29340JS00004BA/20